ALCOHOL
and the
YOUNG

*Report of a joint working party of
the Royal College of Physicians and
the British Paediatric Association*

The Royal College
of Physicians

1995

The Royal College of Physicians acknowledges
the financial support of this publication by
The Jerwood Foundation

Royal College of Physicians of London
11 St Andrews Place, London NW1 4LE

Registered Charity No 210508

Designed and typeset by the Royal College of Physicians Publications Unit

Printed in Great Britain by The Lavenham Press Ltd
Lavenham, Sudbury, Suffolk

P J Graham FRCP FRCPsych (*Chairman*)
Chair, National Children's Bureau. Emeritus Professor of Child Psychiatry, Institute of Child Health, University of London

J O Beattie FRCP (*Honorary Secretary*)
Consultant Paediatrician, Stirling Royal Infirmary, Stirling

E Appleby
Director, Alcohol Concern, London

J Catford DM FRCP FFPHM
Deakin University, Melbourne, Australia

Marion R Crouchman FRCP
Consultant Paediatrician, King's College Hospital, London

Leslie Davidson MD MSc MFPHM, MRCP
Consultant Paediatric Epidemiologist and Hon Senior Lecturer, King's College School of Medicine and Dentistry, London

Christine Eiser BSc PhD
Reader in Health Psychology, Washington Singer Laboratories, University of Exeter

Jane Fortin LLB
Solicitor, and Senior Lecturer in Law, School of Law, King's College London

P Gammage PhD
Dean of the Faculty of Education, University of Nottingham

A H Ghodse FRCP FRCPsych
Head of the Division of Addictive Behaviour, St George's Hospital Medical School, London

Pamela Gillies PhD
Senior Lecturer in Public Health, University Hospital, Nottingham

Gill Hollyn
Hereford & Worcester Alcohol Advisory Service (*until November 1994)

R MacFaul FRCP
Consultant Paediatrician, Pinderfields Hospital, Wakefield, and formerely Honorary Secretary, British Paediatric Association, London (*until November 1994)

D Milligan FRCP
Honorary Assistant Secretary, British Paediatric Association, London (*from December 1994)

Jane Pullin RGN, RMN, BSc (Hons)
Clinical Nurse Specialist, Alcohol Advisory Service, London

H Swadi MRCPsych
Senior Lecturer, Department of Child & Adolescent Psychiatry, United Medical and Dental Schools, Guy's and St Thomas' Hospital, London

P Thorogood
County Director, Hereford & Worcester Alcohol Advisory Service (*from December 1994)

P Wallace FRCGP
Professor of Primary Health Care
Royal Free Hospital School of Medicine, London

D R London DM FRCP
Registrar, Royal College of Physicians

*date of leaving or joining the working party

Observers

Dr A Thorley
Senior Medical Officer, Department of Health

Mrs Annette Young
Social Services Inspector, Department of Health

In attendance
Barbara Coles MA
(Working Party Secretary)

Acknowledgments

The Working Party is grateful to the following for their advice:

Professor M Plant
Director, Alcohol Research Group, Department of Psychiatry, The University of Edinburgh

Ms Eileen Goddard
Office of Population Censuses & Surveys

Dr Chris Power
Institute of Child Health, University of London

Dr John Rae
Director, Portman Group

Mrs Linda Wright
TACADE, Salford

Professor Howard Parker
Department of Social Policy, University of Manchester

Foreword

We hear a great deal in the media about the impact of drugs on children and young people. Certainly many illicit drugs are a worrying threat to their health. But we should not forget that alcohol poses at least as great a menace.

Parents who are problem drinkers and abuse their children, drunk drivers who kill or injure child pedestrians, young people themselves who get involved in drunken fights that result in serious injury to themselves or others, depressed teenagers who attempt or even commit suicide while intoxicated — these are examples of situations in which, looking at the population as a whole, alcohol certainly has at least as great an impact on child health and welfare as illicit drug-taking.

This report reviews the evidence for the extent of the damage alcohol causes the young. Detailed recommendations are made that together represent a coherent strategy for prevention and for the development of treatment services. The Royal College of Physicians and the British Paediatric Association strongly support the recommendations and commend this report to all professionals working with children, young people and their families.

So seriously do we take this problem that our two organisations intend to monitor the impact of the report and review the situation in two years' time to determine whether stronger action needs to be taken.

November 1995

Leslie Turnberg
President, Royal College of Physicians

Roy Meadow
President, British Paediatric Association

Contents

Preface

Alcohol can harm children and young people to an alarming degree. The harm is caused not only by parents and other adults who are problem drinkers, but by excessive consumption among the young themselves. The Royal College of Physicians[1], the Royal College of Psychiatrists[2] and the Royal College of General Practitioners[3,4] have all relatively recently produced reports reviewing the extent and effects of problem drinking in the population. However, none of these reports has provided an adequate account of the ways in which excessive alcohol consumption affects the lives of children. Our report aims to fill this gap.

A summary, followed by our recommendations is placed at the beginning of the report. We then review the extent and effects of problem drinking by parents and the ways in which such drinking should be identified and managed. We go on to describe the extent of drinking and problem drinking by children and young people themselves and the ways in which such problem drinking can be identified and treated. Subsequent chapters deal with proposed preventive measures, implications for professional training and education, and existing gaps in knowledge for which research is urgently required.

This report is intended for a wide audience. The information it contains will be of interest and importance to health professionals, including general practitioners, health visitors, paediatricians, child and general psychiatrists, and also to other professionals, such as teachers, social workers and educational and clinical psychologists, who will find the report relevant to their work. We hope that those in purchasing authorities who are commissioning preventive and treatment services will consider our recommendations carefully and give greater priority to this area of work than has hitherto been the case. Finally, we hope that parents and teenagers themselves — that is those who have the major responsibility for ensuring that drinking alcohol is a pleasurable but not a dangerous activity — will find the report helpful.

November 1995

SUMMARY

Introduction

Drinking alcohol is an accepted part of the social life of the nation. Most adults have at least an occasional drink with friends, and many, apart from those who, for example, abstain for religious reasons, would expect alcohol to be provided at a family celebration, or a party at work. For many too, it is one of the pleasures of life.

Yet, as we know, alcohol can kill and, as described in the four reports mentioned in the preface, among adults can cause very significant ill health and unhappiness, sometimes destroying careers and wrecking family life. Heavy alcohol consumption sometimes begins in adolescence.

Children and young people are born into a world where drinking alcohol is seen as both a pleasure and a danger. Young people count the cost for the future the least, and for most young people the feeling of belonging to the adult world and experiencing the pleasurable effects of alcohol far outweigh concerns for health. Consequently there is a need to protect children and young people from alcohol-related harm. On the other hand, adults are also aware that, in general, the young have an uncomfortable tendency to ignore their messages or even to react against them, particularly when what adults say accords poorly with what they do. Further, the young need encouraging to take responsibility for their own decisions. The molly-coddled child grows into the adolescent who cannot work out limits for himself or herself.

But the fear of paternalism should surely not prevent those who are knowledgeable in this field from providing information that helps the young as well as parents and others looking after children to make more informed choices. Further, when, as is the case with alcohol, an accepted part of our social life can have such dangerous outcomes, costly to the individual and society, government has a responsibility to ensure that it is easier to make good choices than bad ones, and that, for those who do make bad choices and end up as casualties, proper help is provided.

The aims of this report are to assist parents and young people to make good choices, to provide government with information concerning policies that makes those choices easier, and to help professionals in their tasks of prevention and treatment. We begin by outlining the extent of alcohol-related harm among the young and then go on to consider preventive and treatment measures. What follows in this Summary is a synthesis of the full report.

1. Problem drinking by parents

Alcohol can and does affect fertility and increases the risk of spontaneous abortion. Drinking in pregnancy can harm the fetus which is most liable to be damaged in the very early stages of pregnancy. So it is wise for women planning to become pregnant to abstain or drink very little from the time of their period until the first six weeks of their pregnancy, and subsequently to drink only occasionally and well within recommended limits during the rest of the pregnancy. Those who drink moderately or, more especially, heavily around the time of conception risk having babies born with the full or partial fetal alcohol syndrome. While this syndrome may involve many physical abnormalities, mental retardation is the most common and disabling feature.

Parents who drink alcohol excessively cannot supervise their children properly. Consequently their children have an increased risk of accidents, and their physical and emotional needs may be neglected. Furthermore, problem drinking by parents and others looking after children increases the risk of uncontrolled violence and physical abuse within the home. Much domestic violence is carried out when the offender is drunk. Alcohol is sometimes an enabling factor in child sexual abuse.

2. Assessment and management of children of parents with a drinking problem

All professionals, especially those in the health and social services field, have a responsibility to recognise when problem drinking affects peoples capacity to be good parents. Some aspects of unwise drinking, such as somewhat overstepping the recommended limits, will not, of course, in themselves significantly impair parenting. But all professionals have a duty to contact the local social services department if their observations suggest a child is suffering or is likely to suffer significant harm. With this in mind, health professionals working with parents and children need to be able to take a drinking history and to assess the degree to which alcohol might be impairing parenting capacity. They should have the skills to counsel parents to help them to reduce their intake, refer them to appropriate agencies if unsafe drinking continues and, as far as possible in partnership with parents, ensure that adequate child protection measures are taken if the child is at risk of significant harm.

3. Patterns of drinking behaviour in the young: prevalence, influences and impact

Most children in the UK have had their first alcoholic drink by the time they reach their teenage years. This in itself is of little, if any, significance. What is more worrying is the degree to which young people and sometimes children get drunk with a consequent risk of damaging themselves or others. We document evidence of the extent of problem drinking in children and young people. We present evidence from a cross-national study that 13 and 15 year olds in Wales head a list of ten countries in the frequency with which 13 to 15 year olds get drunk, with Scotland not far behind. (The study did not include England.)

After considering the development of 'normal' drinking behaviour, and the background factors related to excessive consumption, we then discuss its effects — the extent to which intoxication in the young increases the risk of road traffic accidents, unsafe sex, and violence. For example, more than one in ten 16 to 19 year old young men drinking under 21 units a week, and more than four in ten drinking over the recommended limits have been involved in a physical fight as a consequence of drinking alcohol.

Finally, we document the degree to which alcohol consumption is sometimes a 'gateway' to consumption of illicit drugs. For many young people, illicit drugs are as accessible as alcohol. The alcohol and drug scenes are closely related and need to be considered together.

4. The assessment and treatment of alcohol problems in the young

After parents, the main responsibility for identifying problem drinking in the young lies in the primary care services, broadly defined to include not only family doctors and practice nurses, but also school nurses, dentists, doctors (to whom teachers should be able to refer readily) and social workers. These professionals should be able to provide effective front line counselling. There should also be a defined multidisciplinary Young People's Alcohol and Drug Service in each district to which referrals can be made. Bearing in mind the reluctance of the young, like older people, to acknowledge their alcohol consumption as causing a problem, such a service would need to pay particular attention to its accessibility, acceptability and sensitivity to local needs and the local pattern of services.

5. Prevention

Alcohol consumption in the young mirrors that in the total population. The number of people suffering from alcohol-related harm is correlated with the annual consumption of the population. Therefore governments motivated to reduce alcohol-related harm in the young (as well as in the rest of the population) will pursue measures to cut total consumption. The single most effective way of achieving this aim is price control through taxation. Other measures play a part, and in our recommendations (see below) relating to prevention, we take into account evidence that suggests that action on advertising, marketing codes of practice, and labelling would have a useful effect. We point to the confused state of our laws on limiting access of young people to alcohol and the degree to which these laws are ignored. We discuss evidence to suggest that the introduction of random breath testing and lower limits of blood alcohol for drivers would further cut alcohol-related road traffic accidents. We point to the lack of sound evidence that health education in schools has much impact on the behaviour of children and young people. While acknowledging the right of children and young people to information and the acquisition of social skills that would enable them to reduce their alcohol intake, we indicate that we believe health education to be an unsafe plank on which to base an entire effective preventive policy.

6. Training

All professionals in touch with children, young people and parents need information on the extent of alcohol-related harm and on means of identifying and treating parents and young people who are at risk. At present, the training of nurses, doctors, social workers, youth workers, teachers, and many other relevant professionals is inadequate. We make recommendations on the core curriculum content in this subject that should form the basis of training, with additional special consideration being given to other issues, depending upon the setting in which the professional group in question will be working.

7. *Research*

Research into alcohol problems in parents and the young is still exceedingly small in relation to the size of the problem and our lack of knowledge on important issues. As examples we note that only limited information is available on the continuity of problem drinking from adolescence to adulthood; that there are no effective screening methods to identify problem drinking in young people in primary care settings, and that we know virtually nothing about the pattern of drinking in second and third generation immigrant families with a tradition of abstinence. We point to the need for a greatly expanded, coherent research programme in this field, with research activity much less dependent than is currently the case on financial support from the drinks industry. We recommend that the NHS Research Directorate takes responsibility for the development of a coordinated research programme.

RECOMMENDATIONS

Introductory statement

The Working Party recognises that many sectors of our society play a role in ensuring that young people adopt a safe approach to the use of alcohol. To each of these we address specific recommendations which we hope will be implemented within their organisations. We also urge people at all levels of society — from children, young people and parents themselves to professionals and to politicians at a national level — to undertake a public advocacy role in favour of safe drinking.

NATIONAL POLICY RECOMMENDATIONS

1. *Annual consumption:* in the light of the fact that the alcohol consumption of young people is a reflection of the consumption of the total population, steps should be taken to ensure that this should not rise above the present level of 9.1 litres of alcohol per person in the population aged over 15 years (equivalent to 2.5 units per day). Further, government should act to reduce annual consumption to about 5 litres (or 1.5 units a day) per head over the next 10 years. (see Chapter 5)

2. *Pricing/taxation:* the real price of alcohol and alcohol products should be regularly increased by taxation in order to achieve a strong price disincentive on alcohol for young people. (see Chapter 5)

3. *Advertising and promotion:* all forms of alcohol sales promotion directed towards the young (including arts and sports sponsorship by alcohol companies) should be subject to tighter regulation. (see Chapter 5)

4. *Marketing codes of practice:* the code of practice for marketing alcohol products to young people should be reviewed in the light of an increasing tendency for alcohol companies to target their products towards the young. In particular, marketing methods which blur the distinction between alcohol and illicit drugs should be banned.

5. *Labelling:* legislation should be introduced that requires alcoholic drinks to be prominently labelled with their alcohol content by units. Alcoholic drinks should also be labelled with recommended limits to assist consumer choice and self-monitoring. (see Chapter 5)

6. *A review of legislation:* there should be a Government review of existing licensing legislation concerning the young with the aim of introducing legislation that is consistent, reduces the risk of alcohol-related harm to children and young people, and is enforceable. (see Chapter 5)

7. *Minimum legal age for sales of alcohol:* current legislation prohibiting sales of alcohol to young people under 18 years should be fully and firmly enforced. (see Chapter 5)

8. *Public houses and children's certificates:* the use of children's certificates should be properly regulated, and their effects monitored.

9. *Licensees:* all licensees should be required to possess the British Institute of Innkeeping Licensee Certificate. In addition, children's licensing certificates should only be issued where trained service/bartenders are present at all times. The age of alcohol servers should not be less than 18 years.

10. *Drunken driving deterrence:* the existing limit of 80mg% should be reviewed.

11. *Learner drivers:* the legal limit of blood alcohol should be reduced to 20mg% for learner drivers and those who have passed their driving test in the previous two years. This is the lowest limit that can be reliably measured, and inexperienced young drivers should be advised not to drink at all before they drive.

PARENTS, CHILDREN AND YOUNG PEOPLE

12. Would-be parents and all young women should be particularly aware of the dangers of alcohol consumption in pregnancy around the time of conception. So it is wise for women planning to become pregnant to abstain or to drink very little from the time of their period until the first six weeks of their pregnancy, and subsequently to drink alcohol only occasionally and well within recommended limits.

13. Parents should be aware of the potential impact of their drinking habits on those of their children, and ensure that their alcohol consumption does not impair their capacity to care for their children properly. (see Chapter 2)

14. Parents whose children drink alcohol should try to ensure that it is consumed in moderate and safe quantities. (see Chapter 3)

15. Parents should try to make opportunities to discuss alcohol consumption with their children in the context of their general health. If they think their child has a drinking problem they should seek help and encourage their child to do so. (see Chapter 3)

16. Parents should be alert to the dangers of allowing their children to drink alcohol unsupervised or in situations where it is potentially dangerous. (see Chapter 3)

17. Children and young people should be aware of the dangers of alcohol abuse. (see Chapter 3)

18. Children and young people should know that it is dangerous to encourage their friends to get drunk or to drink over the recommended limits. (see Chapter 3)

COMMISSIONERS OF HEALTH, EDUCATION AND SOCIAL SERVICES

19. *Monitoring patterns of alcohol use:* levels of alcohol drinking amongst young people at district level should be monitored by health and social services and social care agencies, and published on a regular basis. To this end, purchasers should commission periodic surveys to monitor levels of drinking among the young. (see Chapter 5)

20. *A Young People's Drug and Alcohol Service:* commissioners of health services should ensure that all children and young people in need have access to a multidisciplinary specialist centre for the assessment and management of children and young people — a Young People's Drug and Alcohol Service. They should ensure the service is accessible and relevant to local needs and, when a young person refuses help from it, should be capable of counselling parents and teachers. (see Chapter 4)

21. ***Alcohol education:*** schools should provide opportunities for alcohol education in the personal and social component of the curriculum. (see Chapter 5)

    In particular:-

    ■ Young people should be assisted to resist social and marketing pressures to drink alcohol in excess by being taught appropriate personal and social skills in school;

    ■ Relevant information should be provided to young people on the short-term risks of acute alcohol intoxication, and on longer term health effects of problem drinking;

    ■ Primary and secondary schools should be used as efficient settings for contacting large numbers of young people with educational programmes;

    ■ Family, parents and carers should be involved with teachers in alcohol education to reinforce teaching in the classroom.

PROVIDERS OF HEALTH, EDUCATION AND SOCIAL SERVICES

22. ***Services for adults:*** all professionals should be alert to the possibility that the quality of childcare by parents and others may be impaired in those drinking over the recommended limits. Professionals in the health and social services should, in these circumstances:

    ■ identify parents and others who are caring for children who are drinking unwisely, counsel them about their drinking habits, and work with them to reduce their consumption to within recommended limits

    ■ refer, if necessary, to the appropriate service: GP, psychiatric or substance abuse service, etc.

    ■ refer to the local social services department if there is a suspicion that a child is suffering or is likely to suffer significant harm. (see Chapter 4)

23. ***Services for children and young people:*** all professionals, including especially general practitioners, school nurses and social workers, should be capable of identifying and counselling or, if necessary, referring children and young people who are drinking over the recommended limits, or are otherwise at risk of alcohol-related harm, to the appropriate agencies. (see Chapter 4)

24. ***Prevention:*** all professionals should regard prevention of alcohol harm as part of their work, giving special attention to the periconceptual period in would-be parents, as well as to parents of young children, and to adolescents. (see Chapter 5)

25. ***Health education:*** health education material about alcohol use should be made available in those settings of medical and dental care, youth clubs, schools etc. where young people and parents are likely to see them. (see Chapter 5)

26. ***Drinking on health, education and social services premises:*** as is now commonly the case with smoking control, school, youth club and social service policies on alcohol control should be established and implemented for staff working at these sites as well as for young people attending them. Where a social function involves alcohol consumption, it should be held away from the work place. (see Chapter 5)

27. ***Counselling for professional staff working with young people:*** better training should be provided for a wide range of professionals on the hazards of excessive alcohol consumption, on means of limiting intake, and on appropriate procedures for obtaining help for colleagues who appear to be at risk of alcohol-related harm. (see Chapter 5)

ORGANISATIONS VALIDATING AND UNDERTAKING PROFESSIONAL TRAINING

Professionals for whom this recommendation is relevant include all health professionals, teachers, social workers, the police, probation officers, youth workers, psychotherapists and clinical psychologists.

28. A common core programme relevant to safe drinking should be introduced into the basic training and continuing education of all those working with parents, children and young people. The programme should impart a basic understanding of alcohol, alcohol problems and their management, and how skills relevant to the profession in question can be applied to enable others to consider their own drinking behaviour. (see Chapter 6)

RECREATION AND SPORTS CLUBS FOR YOUNG PEOPLE, YOUTH WORKERS, ETC.

29.   *Sale of alcohol:* on licensed premises where alcohol is sold, the existing laws should be strictly and firmly enforced. (see Chapter 5)

30.   *No-alcohol and low-alcohol drinks:* the sale of no-alcohol and low-alcohol drinks should be encouraged by a policy of low pricing and attractive packaging. (see Chapter 5)

31.   *Dealing with drunkenness in the young:* staff working in licensed premises should be given clear guidelines on the management of young people who are obviously drinking over the recommended limits and/or are intoxicated. (see Chapter 5)

ALCOHOL INDUSTRY

32.   *Availability of low-alcohol drinks:* the availability of low-alcohol drinks in public houses, restaurants and off-licences should be increased, and they should be marketed at more competitive prices in order to increase their attraction. (see Chapter 5)

MAJOR RESEARCH FUNDING BODIES (DEPARTMENT OF HEALTH, MEDICAL RESEARCH COUNCIL AND WELLCOME TRUST)

33.   *An expanded programme of research:* research activity in issues relevant to alcohol and the young should be generally strengthened, and the number of UK centres involved in such activity should be increased. (see Chapter 7)

34.   *Sources of research funding:* research funding in this field should in the main come directly or through contracts from governmental and non-governmental agencies, independent of the alcohol industry. Research funded by the alcohol industry is welcomed, but the industry should not constitute the main source of funding. (see Chapter 7)

35.   *Co-ordinated research programme:* the NHS Research and Development Directorate should initiate a discussion meeting between the relevant government departments and major research funding bodies to establish how research in this neglected and important field of alcohol and the young could be promoted, and appropriate financial resources identified. (see Chapter 7)

1 Problem drinking by parents

FACTS

☐ Two-thirds of newborn babies have been exposed to alcohol at some point during their mother's pregnancy.

☐ Women who drink heavily in pregnancy are also more likely to smoke, use illicit drugs and be socially disadvantaged.

☐ Women who have one or more alcoholic drinks a day in the first three months of pregnancy are twice as likely to have a spontaneous abortion in the second three months than those who abstain from drinking.

☐ The fetus is most vulnerable to the adverse effects of alcohol (fetal alcohol syndrome — FAS, or partial fetal alcohol syndrome — PFAS) in the early weeks of pregnancy, and perhaps before women know they are pregnant. Heavy drinking is dangerous at any time during pregnancy.

☐ Virtually all FAS or partial FAS children show some degree of mental retardation.

☐ Problem drinking in parents is sometimes accompanied by substance abuse, and substance abusing parents are also frequently problem drinkers, making it difficult in some circumstances to disentangle the effects of the two on their children. At any rate, the additional presence of problem drinking significantly increases all risks to children of parents who use illicit drugs.

☐ Studies from the US show greatly increased rates of problem drinking in fathers who physically abuse their children. Though it is difficult to establish causality, in over a third of cases of domestic violence in which children are abused in the home, the offender is drunk.

☐ Rates of problem drinking are raised in parents of children who are sexually abused.

☐ Problem drinking in parents is linked both to poor supervision of toddlers and greater frequency of injury.

☐ Prior consumption of alcohol by drivers is still a major factor in road traffic injuries in which children are killed or traumatised.

☐ Substantial emotional damage is widespread in children of parents who are problem drinkers.

Introduction

From the moment of conception, through pregnancy and the whole of their early years, right through into adolescence, children are vulnerable to the effects of drinking by their parents; obviously the impact of problem drinking is different at different times. During pregnancy the effect on the developing organism is due to physical factors — the toxic effect on the fetus of exposure to alcohol. After birth the effects are indirect, mediated through the social impact of problem drinking on family life and the upbringing of children. In this chapter we review the impact of problem drinking by parents and other adults on the fetus, child and adolescent. (We provide a variety of definitions of problem drinking in Appendix 3).

Alcohol, fertility and abortion

Persistent heavy drinking in men and women produces lasting sexual changes as a result of the direct toxic effects of alcohol on the testes and ovaries.[1] Levels of male sex hormones are reduced in male problem drinkers, and female hormones (eg oestradiol) important in fertility, are reduced in women drinkers. In one study, 39% of a sample of men attending a male infertility clinic were considered to have alcohol-impairment of sperm formation. Semen analysis of half these men returned to normal after three months of alcohol abstinence.[2]

Spontaneous abortion and neonatal deaths are more common where one parent has a major drinking problem. Thus, Nordberg *et al*[3] found that 17% (11 out of 64) of pregnancies in families where one parent was known to be addicted, ended in spontaneous abortion or neonatal death compared with 7% (31 out of 468) of pregnancies in families without a parent with known addiction. Harlap and Shiono[4] found that one or more alcoholic drinks a day in the first three months of pregnancy doubles the rate of spontaneous abortion in the second three months when compared to those who abstain altogether from alcohol.

Effects of alcohol on the fetus

Drinking in pregnancy

Many mothers develop an aversion to alcohol during pregnancy with a spontaneous decrease in alcohol intake or abstinence as pregnancy progresses.[5] However, two-thirds of newborn infants have been exposed to alcohol at some point during pregnancy,[6] and some mothers continue to drink heavily. They are often heavy smokers and have partners who also drink heavily, thus affecting outcome; some also use other illicit drugs which in themselves represent additional risks for the unborn child.

The most serious impact of maternal drinking is the fetal alcohol syndrome (FAS) or the partial fetal alcohol syndrome (PFAS).

Prevalence of the fetal alcohol syndrome

It is difficult to be precise about prevalence of FAS because of uncertainties about diagnosis and because, when the diagnosis is made, it is sometimes unclear whether alcohol is the sole cause because of multiple disadvantages during the pregnancy. There are no reliable UK figures for the prevalence of FAS or PFAS, but figures in the region of 0.3 to 0.5 per 1,000 births have been reasonably reliably reported in the US.[7,8] The lower figure would mean that approximately 200 affected children would be born each year in the UK. Among clearly identified alcohol-dependent women, estimates of FAS following pregnancy vary widely from 2% to 26%.[9] The exact rate probably depends on moderating social, environmental and nutritional factors.[10] While most alcohol-dependent women do not produce babies with FAS, many of their infants may be damaged in other ways, especially in their intellectual development.

Clinical features of children with FAS and PFAS

Diagnosis of FAS is made on the basis of the clinical picture, with supportive evidence coming from a history of maternal drinking.

Neurological development is almost invariably delayed, and intellectual impairment is often associated with behaviour disturbance. Physical problems include poor growth before and after birth, often accompanied by a variety of physical problems such as heart and kidney abnormalities and skeletal defects.[9] Other signs of brain dysfunction, such as clumsiness, tremors and epilepsy may be present.

Mechanisms in production of FAS and PFAS

The precise mechanisms of FAS are unknown. Alcohol and its breakdown products may directly or indirectly interfere with the highly sensitive chemical processes which occur in fetal cells during growth and development. Fetal brain cells may be particularly vulnerable.[11] Accompanying toxic influences, such as heavy smoking and the presence of other drugs, may all interact with the effects of alcohol or otherwise influence the outcome.

Effects of FAS ans PFAS on the child

Infants with FAS have been studied in large numbers into childhood and early adolescence. Although the dysmorphic features (unusual aspects of appearance) seem less marked with time,[12] there are devastating and long-term effects on cognitive function and behaviour.[13,14] Children perform poorly in school and show an extremely high rate (63%) of psychiatric disorders, including hyperkinetic, emotional, eating and speech disorders. Even those children who appear to improve still show severe hyperactivity and behaviour disturbance.[15] The presence of these disorders correlates with the morphological changes, and these in turn correlate with alcohol intake in pregnancy.

Patterns of drinking among parents

It has been estimated that in the United states, about 1 in 8 children have at least one parent who is a problem drinker.[16] Comparable information is not available for the UK. Indeed it is disappointing that despite the availability of findings from several UK epidemiological studies in which the presence of psychiatric disorder in children has been related to other parental mental health problems, there is so little information on parental drinking and problem drinking.

Information about how much people of child rearing age drink would not give a realistic picture of the drinking habits of parents. Within a particular age group parents probably drink less than childless couples who themselves drink less than single people. Nevertheless, it is unfortunately certain that a significant number of children in the UK are being reared in families where one parent is a problem drinker. It is also likely that children from ethnic minority families have an advantage in this respect (see also page 47). For example, the rate of alcohol abuse in Muslim families is extremely low, as it is in first generation Sikh families. The pattern of alcohol consumption in the second generation is, however, unknown, and should be the subject of further enquiry.

Impact of problem drinking by parents on children

There is no doubt that, if one or both of their parents has a drinking problem, children suffer seriously in a variety of ways. However, the influence of other factors in the parent, in the personality of the child, in other aspects of family life, and in the wider environment make it difficult to quantify the precise effects of parental alcohol consumption. We therefore begin with a consideration of the ways in which these factors modify the impact of alcohol.[17,18]

Associated, protective and vulnerability factors

Problem drinkers frequently have other problems. In particular, as far as parenting is concerned, problem drinkers who are parents often have difficult personalities or even personality disorders; their marriages are also frequently disharmonious. Thus violence towards children in a problem drinker with an aggressive personality may result more from the personality or troubled relationships between parents than from the alcohol. These factors may, of course, be related; for example, when alcohol lowers the inhibitions in a potentially aggressive parent.

In these circumstances, the personality disorder is defined as a 'co-morbid' condition. Other conditions found to be co-morbid with problem drinking to a degree greater than chance include anxiety states, depressive disorders and substance abuse; each of them can independently affect parenting to a marked degree.

Children also will possess both vulnerability and protective factors, and in considering the impact of problem drinking in a parent it is necessary to take these into account. Vulnerability factors that increase the risk of behavioural disturbance, learning difficulties, etc in a child with a parent who is a problem drinker include adverse temperamental characteristics, brain dysfunction and chronic physical illness. They also include factors within the family such as a child's conflictive relationship with one or both parents, marital disharmony or the presence of a mental or physical disorder in one or both parents.

Protective factors that *reduce* the risk of behavioural disturbance or learning difficulties in a child with a parent who is a problem drinker include a warm, affectionate relationship with one or both parents, a particularly resilient personality, high achievement in school or in some out-of-school activity, or a close positive relationship with someone outside the immediate family such as a grandparent.

Whenever a link is established between parental problem drinking and adverse characteristics in children, there will always be a query as to whether the link is environmentally or genetically mediated. As far as effects of problem drinking in children of alcoholics is concerned, it is reasonably clear that in Western developed societies both genetic and environmental factors are involved.[19] The relative importance of each of these will largely depend on availability of alcohol and the consumption pattern.

Development and learning

Heavy alcohol consumption or alcohol dependence in one or both parents may affect their children's development in a variety of ways. In particular, care is likely to be inconsistent and impulsive. The unpredictability of parental behaviour and their failure to pay attention to the child may lead to problems in attachment; lack of stimulation because parents are preoccupied with their own problems may delay the child's development.

Insecure patterns of attachment at one year have been reported in infants born to women with high alcohol use before and during pregnancy.[20] Such insecure attachment may later result in difficulties in forming relationships with other children and in achieving autonomy and independence. The play and emotional expression of young children of parents with a drink problem may also be abnormal, and 'a lack of sustained combining of toys, fantasy play and curious exploration' has been observed. These features may be related to the maternal overprotection that has been noted in controlled studies of the quality of parenting in problem drinkers.[21]

Children of problem drinkers studied both in childhood and adulthood reveal cognitive deficits when compared with children of non-drinkers. In pre-school children, deficits on developmental testing have been identified.[3] In older children and adults, such deficits are evident in tasks involving the performance of precise movements, verbal ability, and some aspects of visuo-spatial ability; fewer or no problems have been found in memory tasks, and even in those areas where clear deficits have been found, the mean scores of children of problem drinkers are within the average range.[17] Nevertheless, these cognitive deficits are reflected in higher rates of poor school performance,[22] though the mechanisms involved are uncertain.

Behaviour and emotional problems

Psychiatric disorders in children are determined by a number of different factors. In general, except for autism and attention-deficit disorder, genetic factors are probably of minor importance. The quality of family relationships and of parental care are of central importance. Problem drinking in parents is often accompanied by marital disharmony and sometimes by inconsistent and occasionally abusive child rearing and it is, therefore, not surprising that children of such parents display a high rate of behavioural and emotional disorders.[18]

Children of problem drinkers tend to have low self-esteem and high levels of anxiety and depression — so called internalising disorders. As they grow into adulthood, they are more likely to develop depressive disorders. In childhood they are much more likely to display conduct disorders, characterised by stealing, lying, aggressive behaviour and truanting. It is of particular interest that in one American study this strong association between problem drinking in parents and conduct problems in children remained after the effects of additional substance abuse in parents had been taken into account.[23] Much, perhaps all, of this effect is produced by the link between problem drinking and parental divorce and family violence, and other types of family disruption.[17]

Children of fathers who are problem drinkers complain more often of physical symptoms, including headache, abdominal pain, nausea and tiredness.[24]

The impact of parental problem drinking may differ both in degree and type depending on the age of the child; for example, Velleman and Orford[25] note that it is strongest in young children and less certain in adolescents.

Alcohol and parental violence involving children

Children as witnesses to violence — A recent report has provided vivid descriptions of the ways in which children are exposed to violence in the home.[26] Almost two-thirds of the children of 108 mothers who had themselves suffered domestic violence, had seen their mothers beaten by their partners. The subject is controversial, but a clear idea of the major role that alcohol plays in domestic violence is provided by the 1992 British Crime Survey carried out by the Home Office Research and Planning Unit.[27] In 39% of cases of domestic violence and in 57% of cases of home-based violence (incidents in or around the home but not between family members), the offender was drunk. This survey revealed that domestic violence was more common when children were part of the household than when they were not, perhaps because of the added stress children bring to home life.

Physical abuse — About 4% of children up to the age of 12 years are annually brought to the attention of professional agencies (social services departments or the NSPCC) because of suspected abuse, and 3.5 per thousand are on Child Protection Registers; of these, about 1 in 4 have suffered physical harm and 1 in 8 neglect.[28] The role that alcohol plays in abuse in the UK has been under-researched, but Creighton[29] found that heavy drinking was a stress factor in 1 in 8 child abuse cases identified by the NSPCC. In a study of multi-problem families, Oliver[30] found that 1 in 3 parents in families with at least two abused children were problem drinkers. The link between physical abuse and parental problem drinking has been more extensively investigated in the USA. A review of five American studies carried out between 1968 and 1979 revealed that 1 in 4 physically abused children had fathers who drank excessively.[31] More recently, Chasnoff[32] found that half of all child abuse and neglect cases identified in New York City in 1987 were linked to parental substance abuse, the rate rising to 64% if alcohol abuse was included.

Sexual abuse — Estimates of the prevalence of the sexual abuse of children and adolescents vary widely depending on definitions involved, but it is generally accepted that between 15% and 30% of adult women report an unwanted experience involving sexual contact during childhood.[33] The significance of alcohol as a background factor in sexual abuse has been little investigated in the UK. Elsewhere, the issue has been studied more intensively. In rural New South Wales, Australia, Yellowlees and Kaushik[34] found problem drinking distinctly more prevalent in the parents of children who had been sexually abused than in the general population. In an American prison population,[31] 63% of fathers who had committed incest had been drinking at the time of the abuse.

Safety

Young children of problem drinkers are likely to be poorly supervised and to suffer injuries and poisoning from the accidental ingestion of toxic substances. For example a study of coroners' records (1984–8) carried out by the Child Accident Prevention Trust revealed six separate child fatalities from house fires in which the responsible adults were too drunk to prevent the children from playing with matches or to help them to escape.[35] The Trust, while noting the lack of systematic evidence and the need for further research, reports that anecdotal evidence supports the view that parental problem drinking is a factor contributing to childhood accidents. It would indeed be surprising if problem drinking did not reduce the capacity of parents to supervise their children properly.

The most common cause of death in 1–4 year old children is road traffic accidents, and, in the US, about one-third of all 5–9 year olds killed in such accidents were pedestrians and about 1 in 7 (14.3%) of American drivers involved in fatal road traffic accidents are intoxicated at the time of the accident.[36] In 1993, 18% of drivers/riders in Great Britain killed in road traffic accidents, whose blood alcohol was known, were over the legal limit.[37]

2 Assessment and management of children of problem drinking parents

Introduction

In Chapter 1 we have outlined the ways in which problem drinking in parents puts their children at higher risk for a variety of developmental, behaviour and learning difficulties, as well as for accidents. It follows that professionals in the health, education and social services fields may therefore find themselves in situations where they have to assess the impact on a child of problem drinking in a parent, and decide whether they need to take action. For example, a health visitor may notice that a mother of a two-month old baby smells of drink when she visits in the morning; a teacher may notice that a mother appears regularly the worse for drink when she picks her child up from school at 4 o'clock in the afternoon; a child psychiatrist or paediatrician may elicit from a mother the fact that her partner is frequently drunk and then behaves violently towards her in front of her children; a social worker investigating an allegation of child abuse may be told a similar story.

Assessment

All professionals, if not social workers themselves, have a duty to inform the local social services department if their observations suggest that a child is suffering or is likely to suffer significant harm.

However, there will be circumstances in which professionals are concerned about the levels of alcohol consumption of a parent but will not refer because there is no immediate serious cause for concern in relation to the quality of child rearing. For example, a doctor or nurse who is well aware that a mother is drinking somewhat above the recommended limits, or a teacher who knows that a father has been convicted of a number of drink-drive offences will not, on these grounds alone, wish to refer. Nevertheless, in these and other circumstances where referral to a social services department is inappropriate, the professional needs to show a heightened level of concern for the quality of parental care. For example, a community paediatrician, general practitioner or health visitor in this situation will wish to ensure that developmental examinations are accompanied by more detailed enquiry than may be usual about the behavioural and emotional state of the child. They should be aware that children of alcohol abusive parents are frequently anxious, isolated, and poorly supervised. The older children take on adult responsibilities, and there may be an element of physical neglect or actual abuse. All such children need careful physical examination and monitoring, and specialist assessment of the developmental and emotional sides of their wellbeing is essential.

Further, it is important that in these circumstances health professionals and social workers can elicit a 'drinking history' as well as assess the impact of problem drinking on children, whether this is in terms of acute episodes of drunkenness or of effects of regular drinking over a period of time. As with all other aspects of enquiry into the quality of parental supervision and care, it is important that the professional, when eliciting such information, does not take a censorious attitude and does not leave the parent feeling inadequate or humiliated. Nevertheless, it is also important to obtain information about alcohol intake and, incidentally, drug use if a full picture of the adequacy of child care is to be obtained. All parents know that they should not let alcohol consumption interfere with the care of their children; when this happens, it is not because they intend to neglect their children. It is therefore reasonable to phrase questions in a form such as: 'Do you sometimes find you've had too much to drink and this has affected the way you look after the children?' 'Do you think the amount you drink does affect the children in any way?' Of course this may lead to false denial, but the professional will be alert to other evidence of unduly heavy drinking, such as the presence of large numbers of empty bottles around or greater material hardship than might be expected from the level of income. Swadi[1] provides a useful guide to practice in these circumstances.

When a professional suspects that a child is suffering or is likely to suffer significant harm, it is essential to report that concern to the local social services department together with all relevant information. This raises questions of confidentiality, but it is clear that, even for general practitioners, who may experience strong conflicts of care and duty between child and parents, the child's welfare should always be the first priority. (For further information provided by the Department of Health, British Medical Association and Conference of Medical Royal Colleges, the recent Guidelines on Medical Responsibility should be consulted.[2])

It is beyond the scope of this report to describe in detail either the child protection procedures or the assessment process that should be undertaken when a child is thought to be at risk of significant harm. The assessment process should be multi-agency,[3] and carried out in a structured way over a predetermined period. As far as possible the process should be undertaken in partnership with parents. In the case of parents who are problem drinkers, assessment may well need to involve the substance abuse or psychiatric service as well as other professionals. The nature of the assessment may be different in a pre-school child from that in an older child who may well be able to express his or her own views and wishes. The assessment looks at the two-way relationship between child and parent, the parent's attitude to the role of parenting, influences from family relationships, and potential sources of external support and help. Like other professionals, as part of the full assessment, social workers should be able to elicit a 'drinking history' and to appraise the impact of alcohol consumption on the quality of child care (see above).

Management

Where children are thought to be at risk of neglect or abuse, decisions will need to be taken by the social services department in collaboration with other agencies and, in the case of parents who are problem drinkers, with the substance abuse or psychiatric services. As far as possible parents should be regarded as partners in decision making.

There are a number of specific issues relating to the children of problem drinking parents. Alcohol problems are often treatable, but there is a need to recognise the different timescales of children and adults. The management of the parent's alcohol dependency is long term, but the child needs immediate stability and nurturing and the two may be incompatible. Those who work with the parents may, rightly, be optimistic about the parent giving up alcohol, but services for children have a paramount responsibility to assess the damage likely to accrue to the child in the meantime. It is therefore important to set a time frame around the assessment and management process which reflects the child's needs rather than those of the adult. It should be noted that it is now widely accepted that abusive parents with substance abuse disorders must acknowledge the need for treatment for their disorder, and at least begin to receive it before serious rehabilitative work with the family is likely to be effective.[4]

Responsibilities of social services departments

The Children Act 1989 imposes a number of preventive duties on local authorities through their social services departments, in relation to improving the upbringing of children in their area. Not only should they take reasonable steps to prevent children suffering from ill-treatment and neglect [Schedule 2, para 4(1)], they are also required to take reasonable steps to reduce the need for court proceedings to remove children from their homes into the care of the local authority [Schedule 2, para 7(a)(i) and (iv)]. Similarly, local authorities should take reasonable steps designed to reduce the need for criminal proceedings against young people. Although all these preventive duties are broadly phrased, knowledge of the destructive effects of alcohol abuse on family relationships and the part it plays in causing alcohol related crimes, should lead local authorities to establish 'alcohol awareness' programmes designed to prevent alcohol abuse both by parents and teenagers in their areas.

Local authorities have far more specific and extensive duties to provide a range of family support services to those children and their families in their area who come within the category of families containing 'children in need'. The definition of a 'child in need' is extremely wide and would certainly include a child of alcohol abusing parents if there was a risk to the child's health. It would also certainly include a child indulging in alcohol abuse if the effects were seriously to damage his health.

[Section 17(10) Children Act 1989 provides that a child shall be taken to be in need if: '(a) he is unlikely to achieve or maintain, or to have the opportunity of achieving or maintaining, a reasonable standard of health or development without the provision for him of services by a local authority under this part (of the 1989) Act; (b) his health or development is likely to be significantly impaired, or further impaired without the provision for him of such services; or (c) he is disabled'].

Local authorities are required to identify and assess children in need in their particular area. Having done so, they must safeguard and promote their welfare and, so far as is consistent with that duty, promote their upbringing by their families by 'providing a range and level of services appropriate to those children's needs' [Children Act 1989 s17(1)]. Departments of Social Services depend on the vigilance of professionals from other agencies, such as health visitors and community paediatricians, to identify families with children in this category who may need assistance. The range of family support services envisaged for families containing children in need is very wide. It includes the provision of day care [Children Act 1989 section 18]; suitable accommodation if the child's parents are prevented from providing it [Children Act 1989 section 20] and a further range of services such as: occupational, social, cultural or recreational activities; home help; holiday provision; day centre facilities etc [Children Act 1989 Schedule 2]. Because there is a duty to provide a range and level of services 'appropriate to the child's needs', this duty, though non-specific, should certainly require the availability of alcohol-related services for a family suffering from the problems of alcohol abuse.

3 Patterns of drinking behaviour in the young: prevalence, influences and impact

FACTS

❑ About one in twenty-five 11–15 year old boys and girls drink more than the maximum amount of alcohol recommended for adults.[1]

❑ More than one in five 13 year old boys and more than one in eight 13 year old girls report having been 'very drunk' once or more in the previous year.[2]

❑ Violent behaviour among young teenagers when drunk is common. Around one in three 15 year old boys and one in five 15 year old girls reportedly have got into arguments or fights after drinking.[2]

❑ A considerable proportion of violent offences, both domestic and outside the home, are committed by young people who have been drinking.[3]

❑ There is a strong and consistent association between drinking habits and unsafe sex, especially among heterosexuals.

❑ Heavy alcohol use is often the first step in a substance abusing career.

❑ Adolescents enter coma at a lower level of blood alcohol than do adults.

❑ Although there has been a marked improvement in alcohol-related traffic fatalities involving children and young people over the last decade, a high proportion of traffic fatalities (perhaps about one in six) remain alcohol related.[4]

❑ Suicide in older male teenagers is strongly linked to alcohol abuse. In the United States one in three adolescents who commit suicide is intoxicated at the time of death.[5]

Introduction

Information on the patterns of drinking behaviour in the young in the UK is patchy. There are, however, various sources of information that are particularly valuable, although some may be misleading because they rest on data collected some years ago, and this is a field where the picture can change quite rapidly. The three main sources of national information are:

- A study of adolescent drinking carried out in 1984 by the Office of Population Censuses and Surveys (OPCS, 1986).[6]

- Two reports of surveys carried out by the Health Education Authority (HEA) in which the drinking behaviour and attitudes towards alcohol of 9–15 year olds and 16–19 year olds in 1992 are reported.[1,7]

- Data from a national 1958 birth cohort questioned when they were 16 and 23 years old.[8]

In addition, there are other studies with relevant and sometimes very valuable information, but of a more limited nature. The information provided by these sources is complex; to make it easier to absorb we provide the data in relation to a number of specific questions.

Prevalence of alcohol consumption in the young

■ *When do children start to consume alcohol?*

At 13 years of age 80% of boys and 73% of girls have tasted alcohol. By 15 years 91% of boys and 90% of girls have tasted alcohol and at 17 years the figures are roughly the same, so that young people who are completely abstinent at 15 years largely remain so at 17 years.[6]

■ *How much do young people who do drink actually consume?*

Boys drink, on average, more than girls and older teenagers more than younger ones. The average consumption of 13 year old boys is 8 units per week (4 pints of beer or equivalent) and the average consumption for 15 year old boys is 15 units. The equivalent figures for 13 and 15 year old girls are 6 and 9 units.[6]

■ *What proportion of young people drink over the recommended limits for adults?*

Six per cent of 11–15 year old boys and 5% of 11–15 year old girls drink more per week than the recommended adult limits.[7] The current recommended safe limits for adults are 21 units per week for men and 14 units for women. The working party did not, in fact, feel confident that the recommended limits for adults were in any way appropriate for young people who had not reached physical maturity. Evidence on this matter is lacking, but it would seem reasonable to be cautious in this respect. In the 16 to 19 year age group, 15% of youths and 8% of young women drink more than the recommended adult limits.[7] Although these figures may be regarded as worrying, they are distinctly lower than those in young adults. According to the 1990 Office of Population Censuses and Surveys General Household Survey, 31% of 18–24 year old men and 16% of 18–24 year old women drink more than the weekly recommended limits for adults.

■ What proportion of young people get drunk?

In the earlier OPCS survey, 28% of 13 year old boys and 15% of 13 year old girls reported having been drunk at least once in the previous year, and at 15 years the figures were 55% for boys and 48% for girls.[6] In a study of Scottish 15 and 16 year olds, more than one in three of the boys and more than one in five of the girls reported having been 'very drunk' in the previous six months.[9] In a more recent study in Wales, about 13% of 13 to 14 year old boys and 10% of girls of this age reported having been drunk four or more times. The percentage was 55% and 48% for 15 year old boys and girls.[10]

■ Where and in whose company do the young drink?

Most young people begin to drink alcohol in the home in the company of their parents and other members of the family. As they move into mid-teenage they are more likely to consume with peers in their friends' homes and in pubs, clubs and discos (see page 32).

■ How well does heavy drinking in adolescence predict heavy drinking in young adulthood?

The information on this issue is particularly sketchy. It appears, however, that there are only low overall correlations between consumption in adolescents (16 years) and consumption in young adulthood (23 years).[8] This is because those drinking somewhat more than average at 16 years are quite likely to be drinking somewhat less than average at 23 years and vice versa. However, findings from the National Child Development Study in which 16 year olds were surveyed again when they were 23 years, make it clear that those who drank most, and most frequently, at 16 were most likely to drink most heavily at 23 years.[8] Unfortunately, the sensitivity and specificity of the prediction is too low to be of any real value as far as targeting the heavy drinking 16 year olds, even if the population concerned were co-operative and effective preventive measures directed towards individuals were available.

■ How far is consumption of alcohol in the young a reflection of consumption in older age groups?

Information in population terms is largely lacking on this issue, but as the amount of drinking in teenagers is closely related to the amount their parents drink, it seems reasonable to assume that adolescent consumption closely parallels adult consumption. In the international survey reported by King and Coles,[11] 13 and 15 year olds were asked about their own drinking patterns and whether their fathers drank. In all countries from which information is presented (Austria, Belgium, Canada, Hungary and Spain), when father drank alcohol a higher proportion of young people drank.

■ Is alcohol consumption in the UK generally on the increase?

Alcohol consumption in Western Europe generally declined in the first quarter of this century, was stable between the two world wars, increased markedly (except in France) from 1950 to 1980 and has remained fairly stable since then. Individual alcohol consumption increased in the UK total population between 1970 and 1990 from 5.3 litres to 7.6 litres of alcohol yearly — a rise of 43%.[12]

■ How does alcohol consumption in the young in the UK compare to that in other countries?

Again information is limited. In a recent survey of 11, 13 and 15 year olds in ten mainly European countries including Wales and Scotland (but not other parts of the UK), Welsh young people, followed not far behind by the Scots, headed the league tables at all ages for those who drank at least every week and those who said they had been drunk at least once. The other countries in descending order in the league table were Belgium, Scotland, Spain, Canada, Finland, Sweden, Austria, Hungary and Poland.[11] Another recent study of 11–16 year olds in France, Spain and England found that the mean average consumption of girls (but not boys) was highest in England, and it is tentatively suggested that lower levels of family support in England might account for this difference.[12]

A further relevant statistic relates to the UK position in relation to overall consumption. In a study of alcohol consumption in OECD countries in 1990, Great Britain ranked fifteenth out of 23.[13] However, in terms of percentage increase (43%) over the period 1970–90, Great Britain ranked fourth out of 23. Indeed, if France continues to decline and Great Britain continues to increase consumption to the same degree over the next 20 years, by 2010 the British will be consuming significantly more alcohol than the French (figures derived from Edwards *et al* [13]).

■ How is alcohol consumption linked to smoking and the use and abuse of other drugs?

The short answer is: very closely. This issue is discussed in more detail in the section on other drug use and smoking (page 42).

Background factors in alcohol consumption in the young

The development of 'normal' drinking patterns in adolescence

The consumption of alcohol, beginning at some stage of adolescence, is part of normal expected behaviour in our society. Except in a relatively small section of the population in which for religious or other reasons alcohol consumption is unacceptable, as children grow into their early teens they expect to drink alcohol, and their parents, teachers and friends have the same expectation. These expectations are reinforced by their observation of the behaviour of youngsters slightly older than themselves, and by images they see, for example, on television in scheduled programmes and in advertising slots. Role models and images together imply that consumption of alcohol in moderate quantities is a pleasurable, socially desirable activity.

Perhaps less obviously and also perhaps less acceptably there is an expectation among parents and among youngsters themselves that they will occasionally overstep the mark and drink too much. A very occasional episode of drunkenness in an older teenager is not seen in most families or by youngsters themselves as a tragedy, but more as an amusing event, in which the after effects will teach the experimenting young person a lesson about how much he or she can consume without such discomfort.

In contrast, heavy drinking in the young to a degree that regularly results in drunkenness, or even occasionally results in violent behaviour, is generally regarded as undesirable and unacceptable.

Such heavy drinking is, as we have seen, not uncommon in the teenage years. Further, while the risks of heavy drinking in adolescents persisting into adulthood are not particularly high, the lives of those involved in such behaviour are considerably disrupted at the time, with consequent, sometimes serious ill effects (see below). In a small, but very troublesome minority, heavy drinking in adolescence does persist into adulthood with disastrous consequences for the individual concerned.

We consider below the various factors influencing the occurrence of excessive drinking in adolescence. It is important to recognise that these factors usually do not operate independently but interact with each other. We defer consideration of the role of the law, of the effects of advertising, and of the impact of health education to Chapter 5 in which we discuss these influences in relation to preventive activity.

Gender

We have already seen that boys drink more than girls and get drunk more often than girls. However, the gap is narrowing. The Health Education Authority surveys[1,7] found much smaller differences than the earlier OPCS 1986 study.[6] In Wales, the gender gap between boys and girls who had been drunk four or more times narrowed from 3.9% in 1985–6 to 1.3% in 1989–90;[10] by now, the gap may have disappeared completely.

Socio-economic factors

The Health Education Authority survey found that in the younger age groups (9–15 years) consumption varied rather little between the socio-economic groups, except that children of professional and managerial parents (AB) drank less. However, by 16–19 years, consumption was roughly similar in all socio-economic groups,[7] and by the early 20s it is individuals in the higher socio-economic groups who are more likely to be drinking at risky or unsafe levels.

The fact that drinking in older adolescents varies little by social class or employment status[14] strongly suggests there are two countervailing tendencies: on the one hand, young people who feel excluded from society because they are out of work or in boring, humdrum jobs are more likely to drink heavily than those studying or in interesting occupations; on the other hand, those with more money in their pockets are likely to be able to afford to drink more. This is an area in which better employment prospects and job satisfaction would improve the health of the population — in this context because of its effects on alcohol consumption.

Ethnic status

There has been long standing interest in differences between ethnic minorities in alcohol consumption with, in general, lower rates of problem drinkers in those ethnic groups (eg Greeks, Jews, Italians, Chinese) that socialise their children in moderate drinking patterns within the family.[15] Within the UK it appears that in 9–15 year olds, drinking above the recommended limits is more common in white (4%) than in Asian and Afro-Caribbean children (0.5%).[1] However, there is marked variation between ethnic groups, with rates of consumption being lower in first generation immigrant Asian children and children from Muslim countries. There are now, however, worrying signs that alcohol consumption may be rising markedly and out of control in second generation migrant children exposed to conflicting messages from home and their peers. This is, of course, but one example of the many cultural conflicts that such adolescents experience, but it does merit further study with a view to planning preventive activities.

Parental influences

It is 'accepted wisdom' that parents are an important influence on their children's behaviour and that many good and bad habits are learned from parents. Most of the research into the association between the patterns of drinking of parents and their children tends to focus on the influence of parents who are problem drinkers.[16,17,18] Offspring of alcoholics are approximately five times more likely to develop alcohol-related problems than offspring of non-alcoholics,[19] although the genetic contribution is uncertain. There are, however, other questions to be asked about parental influence on drinking behaviour. In many families, for instance, alcohol is usually consumed only at meal-times and invariably in moderate amounts. How much of a contribution does the parental drinking 'style' make to the drinking style of the younger adolescent, the older adolescent and the young adult? There is little information on this subject. Anecdotal evidence would suggest that parents who drink several cans of lager while watching television in the evening are likely to induce similar behaviour in their teenage children and that this process will also pertain with teenage children of parents who regularly consume a couple of bottles of wine with their evening meal.

Other family factors

Numerous family factors are linked to excessive alcohol consumption in the young[20]: in particular, disharmonious and quarrelsome family relationships, parental mental illness (especially depression and anxiety states), and parental personality disorders (especially of aggressive type). No specific influence of alcohol consumption is likely to be pinpointed in these circumstances, as it will be multi-factorially determined. Others have put emphasis on the domestic ecology, the amount and distribution of space available to the family with a teenager.[21]

Peer influences

As teenagers grow older they continue drinking at home, but extend the range of their drinking first to parties, then to clubs and discos and lastly to pubs. Certainly by the age of 15 years they seem to prefer drinking with friends of their own age to drinking at home.[6] They also develop more positive attitudes to drinking alcohol and are, if anything, less worried about negative effects.[22]

Drinking with friends is more likely to be unrestrained when there is an expectation of high consumption and of rowdy behaviour. If the young person has friends who are already drinking heavily, he or she will be more likely to do the same. Peer influence is, therefore, of major importance in the development of excessive drinking. Factors likely to direct towards restraint in the presence of peer pressure are a positive self-image (not wanting to let oneself down in front of one's family and oneself), a wish not to let drinking affect school work and other studies, especially if these are being pursued reasonably successfully, and an inability to afford much alcohol. Conversely, a poor self-image, academic failure and low pricing of alcoholic drinks are likely to be influences towards excessive drinking.

As young people move through adolescence, so the pattern of their lives, the context in which they live, will change.[23] As a rule they have more money of their own to spend, if they wish, on alcohol. More and more young people develop stable, affectionate relationships with members of the opposite sex and a minority will develop such relationships with members of the same sex. They will often, at this stage, begin to move away from circles in which heavy drinking is the rule and will want to spend their money in other ways. Those who do not develop such relationships will be at greater risk for persistent, heavy drinking.

Behaviour and personality factors

Extravert children and adolescents who are keen to experiment with new experiences are more likely to consume heavily.[24] Their alcohol consumption will be just one reflection of their lifestyle, just as heavy smoking and a tendency to get involved in minor delinquency will be others. In a minority of young, heavy drinkers there will be more worrying symptomatology, reflecting a significant psychiatric or personality disorder. Teenagers with residual forms of the hyperkinetic syndrome or conduct disorders are more likely to be heavy drinkers. In these teenagers and in those with aggressive personality disorders, lack of impulse control and behavioural disinhibition are likely to be common, significant aetiological factors.

Moderating influences

Finally we need to consider those influences that protect against the likelihood of heavy drinking, although they will not always do so. Warm, affectionate relationships between parents and children, a family attitude to alcohol consumption that encourages moderation without excess, a reflective rather than an impulsive personality in the teenager himself or herself, and friends who disapprove of drunkenness, are all likely to be protective.

In addition, looking at the pattern of drinking from a developmental perspective, the formation of stable relationships, especially during mid and late adolescence, exerts a moderating influence on alcohol consumption. The development of stable partnerships and family formation results in reduced consumption between 16 and 23 years, and partnership breakdown increases consumption.[14] Presumably such effects occur because of the influence of stable relationships on the use of recreational time, and on the way young people in different circumstances choose to spend their money.

Effects of drinking on children and young people

We are concerned here particularly with excessive alcohol consumption, but it must be remembered that heavy alcohol use is often not an isolated behaviour. Heavy drinkers are at greater risk for using illicit drugs,[25] and they may also show conduct disorders with anti-social behaviour. Therefore it has been difficult for researchers to separate the impact of alcohol from that of other drug abuse and conduct disorder. Further, it is also difficult to disentangle factors that lead to excessive alcohol use from the impact of such use: for example, low academic achievers are likely to drink heavily, but high alcohol intake also interferes with learning.

Negative consequences of mild drunkenness

In the OPCS study[6] respondents were asked how often in the previous year they had experienced pleasant or unpleasant effects of drinking, or had behaved in an antisocial way after drinking. There is little doubt that drinking alcohol is associated in the majority of adolescents' minds with social enjoyment. The majority of 13 year old drinkers had woken up the next morning feeling that they had had a 'really good time'. About three-quarters of the 17 year olds reported such an experience.

However, some of the more unpleasant effects of heavy drinking were also reported — vomiting, falling over — were more common among boys than girls. Nineteen per cent of the 13 year old boys had been sick after drinking compared to 7% of the girls. Among 17 year olds the proportions increased to 49% among the boys and 13% among the girls. Some of the symptoms of heavy drinking — dizziness, headache, falling over — were as common among the younger adolescents as the older ones, presumably because 'symptoms of these kinds can be provoked in the youngest adolescents by relatively small amounts of alcohol'.[6] Four per cent of 14 year old boys and 9% of girls had felt so ill the day after drinking that they had not gone to school; 20% of 17 year old youths and 6% of 17 year old girls had experience of being so ill following drinking they had not been able to go to work or to school.

The National Survey also provides evidence of drink-related antisocial behaviour by the young themselves.[6] More boys than girls reported getting into fights or incidents of vandalism or illegal driving. Fifteen per cent of 13 year old boys, 19% of 14 year olds and 14% of 17 years old had 'got involved in breaking things'. A similar pattern is noted among the boys for 'getting into an argument or fight' — the proportion increasing from 15% among the 13 year olds to 27% among the 15 year olds and then decreasing to 18–19% among 16 and 17 year olds.

Severe intoxication or poisoning

Young children's and adolescents' metabolism of alcohol and response to intoxication differs from that of adults.[26] Young people more often exhibit hypoglycaemia (low levels of blood sugar)[27] and a disturbance of their body chemistry (a mixed respiratory and metabolic acidosis). At higher blood alcohol levels, both children and adolescents can suffer hypothermia and breathing difficulties, both caused by brain dysfunction.[28] They are more likely to show seizures, perhaps because of their greater tendency to develop low blood sugar.[29] Children and adolescents suffer coma at lower blood alcohol levels than adults. Coma corresponds more closely to peak blood alcohol concentration (BAC) than to other chemical indicators of intoxication.[27] There is some evidence that alcohol intoxication can lead to brain death and stroke in young adults.[30]

During the 19th and first half of the 20th century, ill children were frequently dosed with alcohol and alcohol-containing compounds which occasionally led to accidental intoxication. Alcohol is now excluded from children's medications. Some parents still occasionally use alcohol as a sedative in milk formula, despite this being a criminal offence unless medically prescribed (Children and Young Persons Act, 1933, s5. Appendix I). There is still the risk of accidental intoxication with mouthwash and perfumes[31] which can be fatal.[32]

The setting for acute intoxication among schoolchildren is largely experimental drinking. Peer pressure sometimes leads to forcible drinking and then to intoxication. Student clubs (eg tequila clubs) and drinking competitions are incentives to the young to drink and can sometimes result in toxic overdose which results in loss of consciousness, seizures and occasionally death. Hard-up students are especially vulnerable to 'happy hours' and are indeed often specifically targeted for these.

Injuries

The most important effect of alcohol on the physical health of young adults is in the area of injury, both accidental and non-accidental. Violence by adult problem drinkers was discussed in Chapter 2, but adolescents using alcohol may also be the victims of assault.

Pedestrian injury — One-third of pedestrian fatalities in the United States were intoxicated at the time of death (blood alcohol concentration, BAC ≥ 0.10g/dl). This was true for 16–19 year olds, as well as older people.[33] In the UK, 9.5% of pedestrian fatalities were drink-drive accidents.[4]

Occupant road traffic accidents — Driving skill is impaired at a lower blood alcohol concentration in young people than in adults.[34] This may result from a differential effect of alcohol on adolescents and/or a compound effect of alcohol on inexperienced drivers. The last decade has shown a drop in alcohol-related fatalities in the UK from 1,550 in 1982 to 550 in 1993[35] — a remarkable achievement, but there is clearly some way to go.

Bicycle injuries — The smaller percentage of bicycle fatalities which occur while the rider is intoxicated than of car occupant or pedestrian fatalities may indicate that motor impairment often precludes the very possibility of riding a bicycle.[36]

Education

Educational attainments suffer in alcohol abusing adolescents, and studies often link alcohol abuse to poor scholastic achievement, school-based problem-behaviour, truancy/unemployment, delinquency and relationship problems.[14,37] Heavy alcohol use may result in failure to complete homework and in absence from school, because of hangovers on the 'morning after'. It may also impair concentration and memory function.

Impact on mental health

This is an area in which it is particularly difficult to distinguish cause from effect. Does poor mental health predispose to problem drinking, or does problem drinking cause mental health problems? Longitudinal studies to determine the direction of causation are largely lacking. The best evidence has been obtained from studies of depressive disorder and suicide.

Deykin *et al*[38] found an association between alcohol abuse and major depressive disorder but not with other psychiatric diagnoses. In a suicide study carried out in San Diego, USA, Fowler *et al*[39] found that 53% of young suicides had a principal diagnosis of substance abuse including alcohol. Follow-up studies have shown a higher rate of later suicide[40] and depressive symptoms[41] among substance abusers.

Alcohol abuse is a major risk factor in male teenage suicides. In the United States, one in three adolescents who commit suicide is intoxicated at the time of death.[5] It is likely that the recent increase in suicide rate in older male teenagers is specifically related to a rise in alcohol consumption.[42] Suicide occurring after attempted suicide in young people is associated with alcohol and drug use, and in a significant number of cases of attempted suicide, excessive drinking is an important background factor.[43]

Excessive alcohol consumption is also significantly associated with other mental health problems. Lavik and Onstad[44] found a significant relationship between episodes of 'alcohol intoxication' and bulimia. Eating disorders were present in 30% of young children and teenagers with alcohol problems, while 27% with eating disorders showing evidence of problem drinking. Labouvie[45] found a strong link between coping difficulty and the use of alcohol and cannabis. A Norwegian study[44] revealed higher rates of psychosomatic complaints, anxiety, depression, interpersonal conflict and social dysfunction among drug and alcohol users than controls.

Crime and antisocial behaviour

In Chapter 2 we discussed links between alcohol and domestic violence involving adults. The relationship between more serious types of youth crime and other forms of antisocial behaviour and alcohol use is also well established.[46,47] A working party on 'Young People and Alcohol' convened by the Home Office Standing Conference on Crime Prevention[48] concluded that alcohol was common causal factor in youth crime, particularly crimes involving violence. They cite evidence that '50% of a sample of victims of wounding reported that the offender had been drinking, as did 44% of victims of common assault, and 30% of victims of sexual offences'. They caution against accepting these figures too literally, but conclude nevertheless that 'a significant proportion of violent offences is committed by people who have been drinking'. Fagan *et al*[49] and Hammersley *et al*[50] confirmed the association between delinquency and substance abuse, but suggested that the relationship is skewed; the severity of delinquent behaviour can explain the severity of substance abuse but not vice versa. Alcohol is closely related to violence (aggression and victimisation).[51] The causal nature of the link between drunkenness and violence has been queried on the grounds that for some violent individuals, having too much to drink in the evening is habitual and that therefore, one would expect a high proportion of violent offences to be committed by people in this state. We are not convinced by this view which offends against common sense and is contrary to the almost universal experience that alcohol removes inhibitions against aggression.

Although there are no well-established links between sex offending and alcohol abuse, in 6% of cases of sexual assault by adolescents the offender or victim was using alcohol or drugs at the time of the offence.[52] Furthermore, 12% of adolescent sex offenders fulfilled DSM-III criteria for alcohol abuse.[53]

Unsafe sex

Adolescence is increasingly emerging as a potentially risky period
for unwanted pregnancy and sexually transmitted diseases. As well
as sexual behaviour, an important factor in determining risk is alcohol and drug usage. Studies indicate that teenagers are more likely
to have casual sex and less likely to use condoms when they are
under the influence of these substances. Two-thirds of a sample of
1,152 adolescents aged 16–19 years said that they had regular sexual intercourse. Of those, 64% said that they had sex after drinking
and 15% after drug use. Only 37% always used condoms.[54]

Being more prevalent than drug use, alcohol use is getting particular attention from researchers. Though findings from a North
American study[55] do not support an independent effect, in a large
survey among older adolescents (16–21 year olds) in North
England, McEwan *et al*[56] reported an association between drinking
habits and unsafe sex, especially among heterosexuals. The probability of having unsafe sex (with someone they met for the first time;
with someone known to have many sexual partners; with many partners) was directly related to the intensity of drinking.

Other drug use and smoking

Heavy alcohol use is sometimes a first step in a substance abusing
career. Kandel[57] proposed that, on the basis of longitudinal research
data in the USA, there is a sequence of stages which most drug users
follow. Adolescents at one particular stage of use do not necessarily
move on to the next stage. However, those at a later stage have
usually passed through the earlier ones and usually continue to use
the same drugs they used in the preceeding stage. Four major stages
in the continuum of drug use were identified. They are the use
of (i) beer or wine; (ii) hard liquor or tobacco; (iii) cannabis;
(iv) other illicit drugs. Kandel and Faust[58] indicate that progression
to a higher ranked drug is directly related to the intensity of use at
the prior stage. Adolescents, however, may stop at any stage and not
go further. Donovan and Jessor[59] have identified 'problem use of
alcohol' as an additional stage between the stage of use of cannabis
and that of pills. The role of tobacco and alcohol as 'gateway' drugs
has been confirmed in a 20-year follow-up of a cohort of adolescents.[60] As 'gateway' drugs, tobacco was particularly influential for
women while alcohol was important for men. Progression from
light to heavy smoking and alcohol use increases the probability of
involvement in illicit substance use.[61] In a study of UK 13 year olds,

those who had used any illicit drug were more likely to have tasted alcohol at an earlier age.[62] The more heavily involved an adolescent in alcohol, the greater are the chances of drug use. Among those who drink more than once a week, 34% have used drugs repeatedly, compared to 22% among those who only drink once a week and 2% among those who never drank.[63]

This concept of progression from alcohol to soft drugs to hard drugs may, however, be misleading in relation to recent trends in the UK youth scene. Many young people in their late teens are now recreationally consuming or using illicit drugs or alcohol alternatives on different evenings of the week, depending on the sensations they wish to experience, the amount they have to spend, the preferences of their friends, and their degree of concern about how readily their parents will detect what they have been using or consuming when they go home.[64] In many parts of the country, the use of cannabis, stimulants such as amphetamine and Ecstasy (MDMA — methylene-dioxy-metho-amphetamine) is so widespread that availability is hardly an issue in determining use.[64]

4 The assessment and treatment of alcohol problems in the young

Young problem drinkers fall into three main groups as far as their needs for assessment and treatment are concerned. These groups are by no means completely distinct from one another and, in addition, some young people will move from one group to another with consequent changes in their needs. The groups are:-

Group A Young people who are drinking over the recommended adult limits, but are asymptomatic and not suffering impairment at this stage as a result of their alcohol intake.

Group B Young people who are drinking heavily, are frequently drunk and impaired as a result (eg with frequent hangovers resulting in missing school, being late for work, or not being able to study properly), but who do not have other major problems.

Group C Young people who are drinking heavily and who do have other major problems. At the extreme end there will be those young people who are also using hard drugs, are homeless and separated from their families, involved in prostitution and other delinquent or criminal behaviour, and have major psychiatric disorders. At the less severe end in this group will be those who are also using cannabis and are involved in minor delinquency and frequently get into fights, but are living at home and coping (although perhaps not very well) with employment or their studies.

One common feature of all these groups is that each is likely to include young people who do not see their alcohol intake as a major problem or, in many cases, as a problem at all. For most young individuals, drinking alcohol will be seen as a pleasurable activity with few, if any, drawbacks. This misperception about drawbacks, for such it is, will be a major complicating feature in assessment and treatment.

The requirements for an alcohol service for young people

A comprehensive service for young problem drinkers should meet the needs of all the three groups described above. The service should be:

- open to referrals from a wide range of sources

- acceptable to young people

- accessible without cumbersome administrative procedures

- sensitive to individual needs

- appropriate to local population needs and the local pattern of services

- able to utilise a wide range of relevant skills and facilities, ie is multi-disciplinary

- as effective as current techniques permit, but realistic in its aims

- monitored for quality.

The Health Advisory Service (HAS) is currently engaged in a 'thematic review of purchasing and providing substance misuse services for children and adolescents' and will shortly produce a report which will describe good practice in this area. Although the present report focuses on alcohol consumption, in fact, as we have already indicated (see Chapter 3), young problem drinkers are sometimes substance abusers and vice versa. We therefore think it appropriate that relevant specialist facilities should be named 'Young People's Drug and Alcohol Services'. The HAS report[1] describes the development of a pattern of services in more detail than is provided here, but the general approach is similar.

Primary care for children and adolescents who are problem drinkers

For children and adolescents who are problem drinkers, primary care should be seen as more widely defined than primary health care, which is based in general practice or health centres, although the latter will clearly have a central role. Primary care workers, in this context, should include school nurses and doctors, social workers, those working in relevant voluntary organisations, as well as general practitioners, practice nurses and health visitors. All these professionals should be alert to the possibility that young people are drinking over the recommended limits of alcohol intake for adults, and should be able either to provide first line counselling themselves or, if this is not their role, to refer appropriately to the general practitioner or to a Young People's Drug and Alcohol Service if there is evidence of impairment as a result of alcohol consumption. They should therefore be able to ask relevant questions that will detect impairment if it is present. Although the emphasis in this section is on primary health care in a general practice setting, the principles will be the same wherever the primary care worker is situated.

General practice provides an important setting for opportunistic identification to occur, as between two-thirds and three-quarters of teenagers attend their GP at least once a year.[2] The role of general practice in the identification and treatment of adult problem drinkers has been the subject of a number of studies, and these are of some relevance to adolescents. Adult heavy drinkers have been identified as more likely to attend their general practice than others. There are, however, some difficulties in relying on primary care to deliver intervention services. GPs vary in what they consider safe levels of alcohol consumption[3] and many are reluctant to become involved in alcohol reducing interventions. In one study, only 40% of GPs felt motivated to work with people who drink in a harmful or hazardous way.[4] 'Effective Health Care', a publication by the Nuffield Institute for Health, reported that in a recent survey of 5,000 adults, only 2% reported any discussion in the previous 12 months related to alcohol use with their GP or any member of the practice staff. The proportion of adolescents having any such discussion is likely to be even lower.

The school health service

The role of school nurses and doctors in problem drinking in children and adolescents is insufficiently developed, but could also be of major significance. Teachers are quite likely to know which teenagers are involved in excessive alcohol consumption or drug use, and should be able to discuss problems with the school nurse.

Social services

Many teenagers for whom social workers are providing a service because there are concerns about the quality of parental care, because they are out of control, because they are involved in the criminal justice system, or because they have special needs will be at high risk for problem drinking.

Other voluntary and local authority agencies

Children and young people who are drinking alcohol excessively may be inaccessible through conventional services. They may, however, be prepared to discuss their drinking in the context of other issues where they perceive themselves to be in greater need of help. Examples of such facilities include voluntary or local authority agencies set up to advise young people with housing problems, and agencies providing advice on family planning. Local authority or voluntary agency youth workers attached to clubs for young people or recreational centres may be another point of helpful contact for young people with drinking problems, as may unattached youth workers making contact with teenagers in a variety of settings. Recent guidance to local authority social service staff working in residential children's homes provides useful advice in tackling alcohol problems with this very vulnerable group in residential care.[5]

Methods of identification in primary care

The main requirement for opportunistic identification in primary health care is awareness of the fact that problem drinking is common in adolescence, together with willingness to ask relevant questions. In adults, the use of a questionnaire substantially improved the identification of people with alcohol problems; an 80% increase in the number of patients identified was reported in one study.[6] These questionnaires are not suitable for use with adolescents without modification, but they do provide useful pointers to areas that need enquiry. For example, the recently developed Alcohol Use Disorder Identification Test (AUDIT)[7] asks about frequency of drinking alcohol during the week, number of drinks consumed on a typical day, inability to stop drinking once started, amnesia for the previous evening's events, and whether the individual has hurt anybody while under the influence of alcohol. These are all relevant to adolescents but, in addition, it would be relevant to ask about inability to study, go to school or to work after an evening's drinking, feelings of hopelessness or suicidal depression after drinking, and the use of alcohol to cope with new, difficult social situations. No screening questionnaires with known levels of sensitivity and specificity are available for use with adolescents. Laboratory tests (eg enzyme assays) are also unlikely to be helpful in this age group. However, a brief clinical appraisal is quite feasible.

The two main identification tasks that the primary care professional, wherever situated, needs to achieve successfully, are to find out:

i   Is the young person drinking more than the recommended weekly adult limit (on the uncertain assumption this is also an upper safe limit for adolescents)?

ii Apart from the occurrence of very occasional episodes of drunkenness, is the young person impaired socially, educationally or psychologically by the effects of alcohol consumption?

If the answer to the first question is positive, counselling is required. If the answer to the second question is positive, referral is necessary, preferably to a Young People's Alcohol and Drug Service. If the answer to the second question is affirmative but referral is refused, then, if acceptable, follow-up appointments at primary care level should be made. In addition, the primary care professionals should, if the young person is agreeable, arrange to see the parents or carers who may be extremely worried, to discuss their anxieties.

Intervention at primary care level

There are no known studies evaluating intervention for young problem drinkers in primary care. Studies in the adult population suggest that intervention at primary care level can be effective in reducing the harm of hazardous drinking and should probably also be carried out among young people. Wallace *et al*[8] reported a study involving 909 adult patients who were randomly allocated to either brief intervention or assessment only. The brief intervention included assessment of alcohol consumption, alcohol related problems and dependence, and compared the patients' reported drinking with drinking habits of the general population. Patients were advised of the potential harmful effect of their level of consumption and given an information booklet. At one year follow-up, the intervention group showed a 20.9% greater reduction in alcohol consumption amongst men and 22.4% greater reduction amongst women than in the control group. The reductions were supported by parallel improvements in biological markers of alcohol consumption. The WHO multicentre trial[9] of brief intervention in primary health care was carried out with a similar design. The results showed that male patients receiving simple advice with or without brief counselling reduced their alcohol consumption by 24.1% more than the control group, while women showed a 10.6% greater reduction than the control group. For non-dependent and early cases, studies from the adult population suggest that brief intervention, while costing much less (30-50%), is just as effective as specialist services. At this stage, it is reasonable to assume that a similar approach with adolescents will achieve comparable results.

Organisation of secondary care services

At the present time, as far as we can ascertain, there are virtually *no* appropriate secondary care specialist services for young people with alcohol and drug problems in the UK. However, the recommendations described here have reached the planning stage in some areas.

Those planning services for this group need to take into account various relevant issues:-

i   The motivation of young people impaired by their alcohol consumption and/or drug abuse to receive help is often low or non-existent.

ii   Related problems such as educational failure, conduct disorders, depression, repeated court appearances and social difficulties at home with parents may be at least as prominent as the problem drinking.

iii The facilities and skills of different services, especially the child and adolescent psychiatry service, the substance abuse service, the social services and the forensic psychiatry service may be required to deal with a young person's particular difficulties.

iv   Services need to be relevant to local population needs. A service for inner-city young people, significant numbers of whom are in local authority care or homeless, may need to differ from a service in a locality where most of the youngsters into heavy alcohol or drug use are from middle class, intact families.

v   For young people with multiple problems, aims need to be limited and realistic.

vi   While young people with substance misuse problems may not themselves wish to receive help, their parents and, in some cases, their teachers, may benefit considerably from counselling and support.

Purchasers in each district should identify a specialist service for young people with alcohol and drug problems. To this end, they should request a provider or group of providers to establish a multidisciplinary service. It is to be expected that this service will be based in an existing facility, but it will be necessary for the provider to ascertain that input is available from other relevant services. Thus, for example, if the Young People's Drug and Alcohol Service is situated in the child and family psychiatric clinic, there should be close links with the Substance Abuse Service and the Social Services Department. The Health Advisory Service Report[1] on this subject provides more detailed information for purchasers and providers on this issue.

Assessment

Wherever a Young People's Drug and Alcohol Service is sited, it should be capable of comprehensively assessing the needs of the young problem drinker. It is beyond the scope of this report to describe comprehensive assessment in detail, but the following information is the minimum that will be required:

- A full history of alcohol consumption and drug use.

- The circumstances of consumption, eg alone or in the company of others.

- The psychological needs met by consuming alcohol, eg relief of anxiety and depression.

- The adverse consequences of alcohol use and the degree of dysfunction caused by it.

- General physical health, including where appropriate, laboratory investigations of liver function, etc.

- Psychiatric state, including any other significant behaviour and emotional difficulties.

- Family structure and functioning, especially the quality of relationships with other family members.

- Educational and/or employment status.

- Social life, including friendships and stable intimate relationships.

- Personality strengths, interests, hobbies, etc.

- Motivation for change, insight into present problems.

In obtaining this information, the young person will serve as the main informant, but information from other sources, such as parents, teachers, and other agencies involved will also need to be obtained.

Treatment

A full assessment along the lines described above should produce sufficient information to allow the development of a treatment and care plan in collaboration with the young person himself or herself and, if possible, other family members and other agencies.

Responsibility for implementing the plan should be undertaken by one agency alone, eg the Child and Family Psychiatric Service, Social Services, the Substance Abuse Service or a voluntary agency, but often there will be a need to call on the skills and facilities of more than one of these.

The components of intervention will depend on the needs of the individual and the family, as well as the skills available locally.

The following may be components of a treatment service:-

- Individual counselling or psychotherapy with clearly defined, realistic aims.[10,11,12]

- Communication skills training with the family, linked to cognitive behavioural mood management.[13]

- Family counselling/therapy with the aim of improving family tensions and communication.[14,15]

- Group work carried out along the lines employed with older problem drinkers and substance abusers.[16]

- Rehabilitation with attention to the external support network, education and employment. Voluntary organisations have a part to play, and recently Alcoholics Anonymous has produced useful material targeted towards young problem drinkers.

- A small minority of adolescents will need admitting to a detoxification unit or other residential facility. However, the size of the problem in the UK at the present time in this age group probably makes it unrealistic to plan for separate detoxification or other residential facilities. Occasionally, the use of aversive medication, such as antabuse, may have a useful role even in young people.

Outcome and evaluation

It should not be assumed that the provision of an efficient and effective service will necessarily result in a high proportion of 'cures'. Realistic aims might include:-

- The development of a trusting relationship between the adolescent problem drinker and a professional so that the former feels free to talk about problems in a manner that would otherwise be impossible.

- Completion of an educational training course or period of employment that otherwise looked unlikely.

- Support for parents, so that their own distress about their substance abusing child is contained and does not lead to complete family breakdown with adverse impact on other siblings.

It is important that those involved in purchasing services can be assured that the outcome of the service is monitored in a way that allows realistic achievements to be recognised

5 Prevention

Introduction

Excessive alcohol consumption by parents and by the young themselves puts them, as we have seen in previous chapters, at risk of serious harm. We believe it essential there should be an active preventive policy reflecting an unambiguous commitment to help parents, children and young people make wide choices in their alcohol consumption.

The Ottawa Charter for Health Promotion[1] provides a valuable framework for intervention strategies, which has been used successfully in the report on teenage smoking.[2] The challenges are divided into:

- building healthy public policy
- developing personal skills
- creating supportive environments
- strengthening community action
- reorienting health services

This structure will be used as the basis of this chapter, but first there will be a discussion of the overall policy objective for prevention.

Strategic direction

An effective prevention strategy for young people must be built on a comprehensive strategy for the adult population. Young people's drinking behaviour will follow adults, not vice versa. For this reason the interventions discussed and recommended will inevitably involve and affect adult drinking. Furthermore, because we are concerned with levels of drinking amongst young people, this does not mean that action should only be focused on influencing their behaviour. It is too simplistic to target the victim, one has to recognise the wider social and environmental determinants of young people's drinking and address these directly.

The more a person drinks the greater the risk of incurring an alcohol-related problem. This is true even though at low levels of intake there is a reduced risk of coronary heart disease. But there is also convincing research evidence that the overall level of a population's drinking is significantly related to the level of alcohol-related problems which that population will experience.

For example, a one litre increase in per capita consumption of alcohol per year will be reflected in a 1% increase in mortality amongst middle-aged men.[3] Consumption is also positively related to suicide[4] and to violence to others.[5] Unfortunately, there appear to be no practical strategies that can influence the population distribution of drinkers without affecting the mean consumption.

What is also clear is that an increase in per capita consumption will be followed by an increase in drinking across the whole drinking population, including the young, together with an increase in the number of heavy drinkers. It appears that the drinking population behaves as one system rather than as several different parts. Increase or decrease in overall consumption is, therefore, likely to result in shifts across all bands of drinking. For that reason the policy target should not be limited to controlling the 'alcoholic' or alcohol abuser. This is merely the tip of the iceberg and it is the body of the iceberg that creates the tip.

Thus, an important objective for controlling the effects of alcohol misuse in the young, as well as the old, is to stabilise and then reduce the per capita consumption of alcohol for the whole population. We therefore recommend that:

> **The annual consumption of pure alcohol equivalent for the total population should not be allowed to rise above the present level of 9.1 litres per head of the over 15 years old population (equivalent to 3 units of alcoholic drinks per day), and the steps outlined in this report should be taken by both the public and government to reduce annual consumption to about 5 litres (or 2 units a day) per head over the next ten years.**

We see no reason why the population cannot enjoy drinking within these targets nor why the drinks industry cannot continue to prosper. Indeed, the increased uptake of higher quality low- and no-alcohol drinks, together with more 'added value' from alcoholic beverages should offer the industry further growth potential and the consumer greater benefits.

It is with this strategic direction in mind that a range of intervention measures can be considered which have special relevance to reducing alcohol related harm to the young. However, a recurring theme of earlier chapters of this report is the close association with other forms of substance misuse, particularly drugs and tobacco.

Alcohol is part and parcel of the drugs culture amongst our youth of today; it is both a 'gateway' substance to serious drug addition as well as a concomitant agent.

Prevention strategies for alcohol misuse should not, therefore, be taken in isolation to measures designed to reduce other forms of substance abuse. Integration of policy, service and education measures should be the hallmark of future action.

Building healthy public policy

Table 1 summarises the main intervention strategies that are recommended for reducing young people's drinking through building healthy public policy.

Controlling price

The most effective way that government can influence the consumption of alcohol is through price. Taxation is a very powerful public health measure.[6] Econometric analyses from a wide number of countries have consistently shown that when other factors remain unchanged, a rise in price has generally led to a drop in consumption. Similarly, a decrease in price has usually led to a rise in consumption. A recent study from the Centre for Health Economics has shown that price increases are particularly likely to reduce alcohol consumption in 16–34 year olds.[7]

Alcohol, therefore, like other commodities, appears to be subject to economic laws of supply and demand. The demand for the product responds to the actual retail cost to the consumer. This is even more important for children and young people who are likely to have limited disposable income. Maintaining a strong price disincentive is a most important preventive strategy. Although objections are raised against such measures, careful analysis shows that they cannot be substantiated if the public health is to be safeguarded. The impact of tax harmonisation within the European Union, with the likelihood that taxes may fall, is, therefore, a worrying feature and should be resisted. There is currently virtually unrestricted access to cheap alcohol imported into southern England, and it would be highly desirable for measures to be taken to close this loophole, damaging as it is to the health of children and young people.

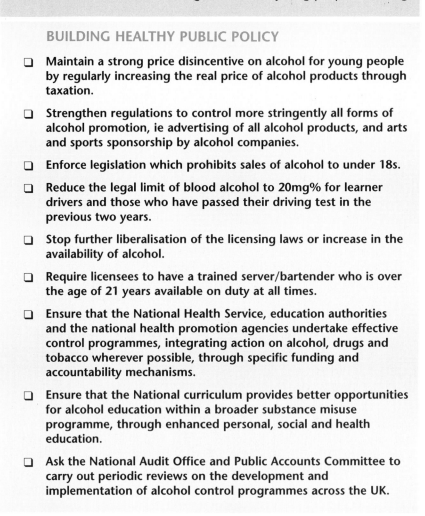

Table 1
Recommended intervention strategies to reduce young people's drinking:

BUILDING HEALTHY PUBLIC POLICY

❑ Maintain a strong price disincentive on alcohol for young people by regularly increasing the real price of alcohol products through taxation.

❑ Strengthen regulations to control more stringently all forms of alcohol promotion, ie advertising of all alcohol products, and arts and sports sponsorship by alcohol companies.

❑ Enforce legislation which prohibits sales of alcohol to under 18s.

❑ Reduce the legal limit of blood alcohol to 20mg% for learner drivers and those who have passed their driving test in the previous two years.

❑ Stop further liberalisation of the licensing laws or increase in the availability of alcohol.

❑ Require licensees to have a trained server/bartender who is over the age of 21 years available on duty at all times.

❑ Ensure that the National Health Service, education authorities and the national health promotion agencies undertake effective control programmes, integrating action on alcohol, drugs and tobacco wherever possible, through specific funding and accountability mechanisms.

❑ Ensure that the National curriculum provides better opportunities for alcohol education within a broader substance misuse programme, through enhanced personal, social and health education.

❑ Ask the National Audit Office and Public Accounts Committee to carry out periodic reviews on the development and implementation of alcohol control programmes across the UK.

Curbing advertising

Alcohol is one of the most widely advertised products in the United Kingdom. Advertising promotes pro-alcohol attitudes and the intention to drink. It may increase drinking among current users and discourage heavy users from cutting back; it may also influence the environment in which public policy on alcohol is formed.

A significant amount of advertising is specifically targeted towards the young, and links alcohol with illicit drug use. The marketing director of Inter-continental Brands reported in *Off-licence*

News (17 March 1994) on his strategy in marketing 'Ravers' a range of six coloured fruit-flavoured wine drinks, four of which contained vodka and two white rum. 'What came out in research,' he said, 'was that the kids thought it (the name "Ravers") was anti-establishment. I think this brand is going to widen the market'. Promotional posters and merchandise, including jackets and T-shirts, are being produced for the trade. He thought the size of this sector of the drinks industry (flavoured, fortified wine drinks) was around £40 million a year.

Because of concerns about advertising, public health researchers have carried out quite extensive studies to investigate the case for regulating alcohol advertising. Three studies of teenagers and young adults have been carried out and all have found small but significant relationships between exposure to alcohol advertising and higher levels of self-reported consumption, and relevant attitudes.[8,9,10,11]

In a recent United States study, of children aged 10–14 years, those who could correctly identify more beer advertisements, held more favourable beliefs about drinking and indicated that they would drink more frequently as adults.[12] One longitudinal study has investigated the relationship between recall of alcohol advertising and alcohol consumption at a later age.[13] This found a significant relationship between the number of alcohol advertisements recalled by 13 year old New Zealand boys and their self-reported beer consumption at age 18.[13]

In the UK, a survey by MORI in August 1990 for the Health Education Authority of young adults' (16–19) lifestyles showed that 37% agreed that 'beer/lager adverts are usually aimed at people of my age' (these represent 48% of 16–19 year old males drinking above recommended limits). Twenty-five percent agreed that 'some beer/lager ads make you want to buy that brand' (31% of those drinking in excess of recommended limits); 82% agreed that 'beer/lager ads should provide more warning about the dangers of alcohol'.

In summary, advertising has a small but contributory impact on drinking behaviour. Public policy to restrict advertising and commercial sponsorship, therefore, remains important and attempts to liberalise it should be resisted.

Limiting access

Most countries have some form of regulation on the minimum age for purchasing alcohol. Age levels vary as does the vigilance of enforcement. Several countries and states (notably in North America) have changed their limits and this has enabled a number of studies of decreased and increased age of purchase to be undertaken. These have generally found that lowering the age limit produced more alcohol-involved traffic crashes for the age groups affected by the change, while higher age limits reduced such crashes.[14] The US General Accounting Office (GAO) reviewed 14 studies[15] which met its strict methodological criteria: four looked at fatal crashes across several states, and five examined fatal crashes in individual states. Reports using data both from individual states and multiple states where the legal age for alcohol purchase had been raised showed reductions in alcohol-involved crashes for young drivers of from 5% to 28%. The GAO concluded that there was solid scientific evidence that increasing the minimum age for purchasing alcohol reduced the number of alcohol-involved traffic crashes for young people who are below 21 years old.

We therefore recommend that the current legislation prohibiting the sale of alcohol to under 18 year olds should be fully and firmly enforced.

Rationalising drinking ages

In Appendix I we describe the present situation in the UK in relation to the law and young people and alcohol.

The law has little influence on the drinking habits of teenagers. Although the law does not prevent young people over 14 being in the bar of licensed premises, it is illegal for any teenager under the age of 18 either to buy, be supplied with, or consume alcohol in the bar (they may drink beer, cider and perry with a meal in a drinking room or separate eating area — see Appendix 1). Despite this, by the time they reach 17, the majority indicate that they are drinking in pubs.[16] More than half of these older teenagers claim never to have been denied service and two-thirds of those who were denied service say this happened on only one occasion. Moreover, substantial numbers of younger teenagers drink in pubs long before they reach that age: a quarter of 14 year olds in England and Wales, rising to 40% by the time they reach 16.[16] It appears that these younger teenagers do not find it difficult to obtain alcohol even though the law prohibits adults buying or attempting to buy alcohol for them to consume on licensed premises and despite the tightening of the licensing law on under-age drinking in 1988. Overall the conviction rates under the licensing legislation for the sale and purchase of alcohol in relation to under-age drinking remain extremely low and are completely inconsistent with the high level of under-age drinking in pubs reported by the young people themselves (see Home Office Statistical Bulletin (1984) Table 5: *persons found guilty or cautioned for offences involving under-age drinking under the Licensing Act 1964*) shows that in 1992 only 34 persons under 18 were found guilty of buying alcohol; and only 87 were found guilty of selling alcohol to persons under 18.) There was a small though short-lived increase in the number of licensees convicted for sales to under-age drinkers following implementation of the 1988 Licensing Act, which imposed on landlords the responsibility for discovering whether teenagers are over 18 and thus entitled to drink in their bars (see Appendix I). Moreover, other teenagers of any age may drink perfectly lawfully in registered clubs (see Appendix I and Reference 17).

The government hopes that the new certification of certain bar premises as suitable for children under 14 years who are accompanied by their parents or other adults, will not result in any relaxation in the laws of under-age drinking;[18] indeed, the new provisions require meals and non-alcoholic drinks to be served in the certificated areas (Deregulation and Contracting-out Act 1994, Schedule 7, para 4, see Appendix I). Nevertheless, it is arguable that as a result of certification, more young people will inevitably be exposed to the facilities and atmosphere of bars at a younger age than before. The impact of this new, important legislation requires careful monitoring, as there is a possibility that it may lead to more, rather than, as is intended, less under-age drinking. It is clear from the above that UK law in relation to young people and alcohol is grossly inconsistent, and, in many respects, is not being enforced.

We recommend that there should be a government review of existing legislation with the aim of introducing legislation that is consistent, reduces the risk of alcohol-related harm to children and young people, and is enforceable.

Deterring drinking and driving

Accidents are the commonest cause of death in children and young people and account for by far the greatest number of life years lost. Road accidents due to drinking are a major factor and adolescents are particularly at risk.

Young drinkers who drive are at risk due both to their inexperienced driving and their inexperienced drinking. One logical countermeasure is, therefore, to establish lower levels for young drivers. Early evaluation of an Australian zero blood alcohol limit (BAC) limit for first-year drivers found that night-time and weekend crashes were reduced.[19] In Maine (USA) Hingson et al[20A] found that a 20mg per cent BAC limit for young drivers produced a reduction in self-reported non-fatal crashes and in actual injury and fatal crashes. A later evaluation by Hingson et al[20B] of the Maine law found similar results, but observed that the enforcement of the BAC law was sporadic. We recommend that a lower limit of 20mg per cent should be introduced for learner drivers and those who have passed their test within the last two years.

While random breath testing has enjoyed limited application in a few European countries with some success, for example in France, Australia was the first country to implement random testing on a wide scale.[21] A high rate of testing, together with a BAC limit of 50mg per cent increased the perception of risk among Australian drinking drivers. The result was that fatal crash levels dropped 22%, while alcohol-involved traffic crashes dropped 36% and remained at this level for over four years.[21,22]

The purpose of random breath testing is not primarily to detect but to deter. For example, in the Netherlands the implementation of experimental random breath testing resulted in fewer drivers with alcohol in their blood, especially of drivers with BAC levels above 50mg per cent, the national legal limit.[23] Experience from other countries indicates that for this measure to be effective the public must feel that there is a high chance of being breathalysed.[24]

Creating supportive environments

Table 2 summarises the main intervention strategies that are recommended for reducing young people's drinking through creating supportive environments.

Changing public attitudes

Public attitudes on alcohol are formed by a combination of what people feel about drinking, what they know about alcohol-related problems, and how they deal with them. Many influences are likely to bear on shaping this social climate. For example, health education through the mass media or schools can raise the agenda that alcohol misuse is of public concern. However, expenditure on alcohol education in schools may signal public concern about alcohol, but may also communicate the message that change will be achieved through individual effort rather than through public policies.

Pressure groups have an important role in setting the agenda for

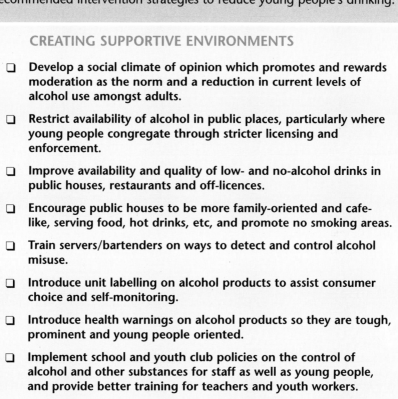

Table 2
Recommended intervention strategies to reduce young people's drinking:

CREATING SUPPORTIVE ENVIRONMENTS

❏ Develop a social climate of opinion which promotes and rewards moderation as the norm and a reduction in current levels of alcohol use amongst adults.

❏ Restrict availability of alcohol in public places, particularly where young people congregate through stricter licensing and enforcement.

❏ Improve availability and quality of low- and no-alcohol drinks in public houses, restaurants and off-licences.

❏ Encourage public houses to be more family-oriented and cafe-like, serving food, hot drinks, etc, and promote no smoking areas.

❏ Train servers/bartenders on ways to detect and control alcohol misuse.

❏ Introduce unit labelling on alcohol products to assist consumer choice and self-monitoring.

❏ Introduce health warnings on alcohol products so they are tough, prominent and young people oriented.

❏ Implement school and youth club policies on the control of alcohol and other substances for staff as well as young people, and provide better training for teachers and youth workers.

policy makers and the public. This has led to the establishment of a number of 'pressure' or advocacy groups on alcohol in Britain and elsewhere. Their aim has been to engage in concerted actions which would achieve high media coverage on key alcohol policy issues. For example, the Royal College of Physicians stimulated the setting up of Action on Alcohol Abuse (Triple A) which was modelled on Action on Smoking and Health (ASH). After some initial successes it could unfortunately not be sustained due to financial difficulties and lack of government support, and was wound up in the late 1980s.

Labelling alcohol content

Warning labels indicating the alcohol content by units, and about the effect of alcohol on health has been used in the last decade in the United States and have had positive effects. For example, Greenfield *et al*[25] found that six months after they began to be used, 25% of those surveyed reported having seen a label. Heavier drinkers who also drove after drinking were more likely to recall the drink-drive warning, and to report taking steps to avoid driving while intoxicated. The increase in self-reported behaviour was in contrast to a decline in Ontario, Canada, where labels were not introduced.

Pregnant women also showed some decrease in self-reported drinking 7 months after the introduction of the warning labels.[26] Much of the evidence suggests no change in the perception of risk, and only some results suggest behaviour change which might be attributed to the warning labels.[27] Nevertheless, it seems prudent to introduce clear health warnings on alcohol products that are orientated towards young people. There has been little evaluation of the effects of introducing unit labelling on bottles and other alcohol containers, but it is reasonable to assume that the availability of such information in a readily accessible form would help consumers drink sensibly.

Changing alcohol content

The availability of different strengths of alcohol product also seems to be important. For example, when wine stores are opened or wine retail monopolies eliminated, wine consumption increases.[28] Even though some substitution occurs, the overall effect is a net increase in alcohol consumption. Similarly, the introduction of medium- or high-alcohol content beer in countries such as Sweden, Norway, and Finland appears to be related to an increase in alcohol consumption.

For example, in an experiment in Sweden strong beer (greater than 3.6% alcohol by weight), began to be sold in grocery stores and in bars in two counties in 1967. The consumption of strong beer increased sharply and that of medium beer declined, while no effect was observed in wine and distilled spirits. The increase in overall alcohol consumption was estimated to be 5%.[29] Assaults were 32% higher and the largest increase in violent crimes was amongst 15–17 year olds.[5] The experiment was terminated in July 1968, in response to complaints by citizens and reports about excessive and inappropriate consumption of strong beer, especially by young people.

At the other end of the spectrum has been the introduction of alternative drinks that look and taste like alcoholic beverages, but have no- or low-alcohol content (eg less than 2% alcohol per volume). The benefits appear promising, although their sales in the UK are very low in relation to drinks with higher alcohol content and are not increasing. Denney[30] found that it was not possible for people to become intoxicated with British low-alcohol beers and lagers (0.5% to 1.2% per volume) using a threshold of the UK legal limit for driving of 80mg% BAC. It seems, therefore, that the availability and promotion of low- or no-alcohol content drinks reduces the opportunity to reach high blood alcohol levels and should form part of an effective prevention strategy. One way to encourage a switch to these products could be through a financial incentive of lower taxation and hence lower prices.

Limiting access

Since the work of Brun et al,[31] many studies have been undertaken to test the importance of limiting physical access to alcohol. Curbs on the number of alcohol outlets and their location have been implemented in various countries, including restrictions on outlets near schools or workplaces. Early studies of density suggested that this factor had little effect on alcohol consumption. However, more recent studies have demonstrated that geographical density does have a significant effect on alcohol sales.[6] For example, Godfrey[32] found evidence that in Great Britain the number of outlets influences the retail sale of wine and spirits; outlet density also increased both the sale and individual consumption of beer.

Most of the studies of changes in hours of sale and opening days for alcohol outlets have demonstrated increased drinking associated with longer hours of sale and less drinking with fewer opening days, together with associated changes in alcohol problems. Research has been conducted in Australia,[33] Sweden,[34] Norway,[35] Finland.[36] One descriptive study on the impact of extended opening hours for Scottish public houses and hotels has also been published.[37] Although containing some methodological shortcomings, these studies present at least descriptive evidence for the impact of these changes upon a number of alcohol-related problems. Indeed, some local authorities have taken advantage of the powers granted to them by the Home Office to adopt bye-laws which restrict consumption of alcohol in public places where young people congregate.

In conclusion, there is strong research evidence to support the use of environmental measures which influence physical access to alcohol. These include not just setting a minimum legal drinking age, but also restricting the hours or days of sale as well as the number, type or location of sales outlets. Such measures should form a major platform of a coherent alcohol policy which seeks to limit consumption by structuring the alcohol market.

Improving alcohol service

Interventions which have encouraged servers of alcohol to act more responsibly have been shown to reduce the alcohol impairment levels of customers leaving bars and restaurants, and the number of alcohol-involved traffic crashes.[38] This has been a popular policy recently in North America, Australia, and the Netherlands, and coupled with server training, should be introduced into the UK. Servers need to have reached a reasonable level of maturity, and the practice of employing under-21 year olds in this capacity should be strongly discouraged.

Server training appears most effective when coupled with a change in the serving and sales practices of the licensed establishment, and with training for establishment managers.[39] A recent study in Oregon, where server training is compulsory for all persons who sell alcohol, has shown that there was a statistically significant reduction in alcohol-involved traffic crashes when at least 50% of servers had completed training.[40]

Making landlords liable for damages if they serve an intoxicated person with resultant personal loss or injury has also been proposed as a preventive policy.[41] Wagenaar and Holder[42] found that in Texas there was a 6% decline in traffic crashes involving injury following the filing of two major liability suits.

Strengthening community action

Table 3 summarises the main intervention strategies that are recommended for reducing young people's drinking through strengthening community action.

Involving the entire community

A central plank of health promotion practice is to strengthen community action by mobilising the considerable resources that are available within communities.[1] This is a broad concept and includes integrating actions from a variety of sectors and settings (intersectoral action), including the full involvement of relevant community groups and organisations.

Table 3
Recommended intervention strategies to reduce young people's drinking:

STRENGTHENING COMMUNITY ACTION

❑ **Undertake local, regional and national mass media campaigns which encourage participation and include advocacy elements.**

❑ **Utilise informal settings to reinforce and support action (eg in youth clubs, leisure centres).**

❑ **Encourage young people to participate actively in alcohol and other substance misuse control activities, eg through health 'clubs', competitions, advocacy work.**

In New Zealand, a media advocacy programme successfully stimulated support for key public policies concerning alcohol availability, advertising, and pricing.[43,44] A similar result was found in Canada with influence on policy regarding the availability of alcohol in recreational spaces.[45]

In Boston, USA a community action project was targeted at reducing alcohol-related harm in road accidents.[46] This intervention included citizen 'policing', school health education, public information areas, enforcement of drink driving and other traffic laws, and training programmes for servers of alcohol. Overall, the six community intervention cities experienced a 20% greater decline in fatal crashes, compared with the rest of the State.

The available evidence suggests then that community action approaches could help to reduce alcohol problems. In terms of controlling the impact of alcohol on young people, the acceptance and backing of the wider community is essential if there is to be further progress in developing and implementing public policies. This also means that young people themselves should participate.

Using the mass media appropriately

The use of the mass media has often been a popular strategy in health education and the alcohol field has been no exception. The content has included promoting 'moderate' alcohol use by switching to low- or no-alcohol beverages;[47] highlighting impaired sexual performance as a result of intoxication or chronic use,[48] and portraying the positive benefits for sporting ability and sexual attractiveness.[49]

Many countries, including the UK, have promoted specific levels of alcohol intake for sensible and even safe drinking. Drinking and driving campaigns have been common, particularly in the US.[50] However, expenditure on such campaigns has never remotely approached the budgets for alcohol advertising by the industry.

Overall, the results of evaluations of stand-alone mass media campaigns have been disappointing, but encouraging results are found when the mass media work is a planned component of a broader community-based strategy, as indicated above with the Boston 'Saving Lives Program'.[46] There is also some evidence of a small effect on alcohol use among teenage school children when mass media messages are combined with a school-based programme, including homework which aimed to involve parents.[51]

One of the drawbacks with the evaluation of mass media campaigns to date has been that quasi-experimental designs have been used. These have tended to look at relatively short time periods, with the consequence that the synergistic effects of other interventions and campaigns over longer periods have been ignored. Nevertheless, probably the most useful role that the mass media can play is in influencing public attitudes, legitimising community action, and developing a positive social climate which supports policy changes.

Developing personal skills

Table 4 summarises the main intervention strategies that are recommended for reducing young people's drinking through developing personal skills.

Responsibilities of parents and young people themselves

We have already summarised the abundant evidence that parents have a major influence on the pattern of alcohol consumption in their children. We believe that parents who themselves drink alcohol should do so in a manner that both provides a model of wise and safe drinking to their children and which does not impair their capacity to care for their children properly. Parents who allow their children to drink alcohol should ensure that it is consumed in moderate and safe quantities.

Parents should not allow children under the age of 18 years to drink alcohol in the home unsupervised, and should adopt a 'no alcohol' policy for unsupervised under-18s parties. In addition, parents should discourage children under the age of 18 years from

Table 4
Recommended intervention strategies to reduce young people's drinking to sensible limits:

DEVELOPING PERSONAL SKILLS

- ❑ Ensure that educational approaches underpin and support lead actions concerning policy development, environmental support and community action.

- ❑ Assist young people to resist the social and marketing pressures to misuse alcohol and other substances by teaching appropriate personal and social skills in schools.

- ❑ Provide relevant information on the short-term impact of teenage alcohol on appearance and cost, as well as health.

- ❑ Target programmes to match the stage of development of the alcohol habit, using new and innovative teaching methods.

- ❑ Use primary and secondary schools as an efficient setting for contacting large numbers of young people with educational programmes.

- ❑ Combine different methods of communication, incorporating personal, group, and mass media methods to reach high risk groups.

- ❑ Involve the family and parents in education programmes concerning alcohol as well as other substances to reinforce teaching in the classroom.

- ❑ Integrate action on alcohol with other educational initiatives to reduce the consumption of tobacco and drugs.

going to parties in other people's homes where alcohol is consumed, unless a responsible adult is present whom they are confident can prevent unsafe drinking.

But children and young people themselves need to take a responsible attitude to their pattern of drinking alcohol. As they become more autonomous, they should take responsibility for keeping their own alcohol consumption within safe limits. They should not allow themselves to be pressurised by friends into drinking above safe limits and should develop the necessary skills to do this. Children and young people should know that it is dangerous to encourage their friends to get drunk or to drink over the recommended limits.

School health education

In Britain more resources have been spent on educational approaches to control alcohol misuse amongst the young than on any other preventive action. School-based alcohol education programmes have been particularly widespread and popular. Earlier efforts were based primarily on the knowledge/attitude/behaviour model, and subsequently included social competency training of various sorts. Interventions have been targeted at the presumed influences on drinking (peer and parental behaviour, and the mass media).

Skills training to assist in resisting pressures to use alcohol and drugs have also been undertaken, including rehearsals of how to say 'no'.[52,53] More general life skills approaches have included self-esteem enhancement, stress management, assertiveness training, values clarification and decision making.[54]

Unfortunately, results of evaluations of such educational programmes organised in primary and secondary schools in the 1980s are not encouraging. Moskowitz[55] found that whereas many programmes were successful in increasing knowledge, very few influenced attitudes, and even fewer affected consumption. One of the difficulties of research in this area has been the failure to address the important environmental influences on health behaviour. Most of the interventions evaluated were operating in a policy vacuum and where environmental influences were at the best neutral or most likely hostile. Perhaps, therefore, it was not surprising that the results were disappointing. Follow-up was also rather short-term. Their longer-term efficacy is difficult to investigate, but any benefit is perhaps more likely to be indirect and come about through heightened political and public awareness.[6]

Educational approaches should, therefore, *not* form a lead approach on their own in combating alcohol misuse amongst young people. There is insufficient research evidence to support it, no matter how attractive it might be politically. The continued investment on school-based education or mass media public education campaigns cannot be justified unless they are placed in a broader context of policy development, environmental control and community action. The same recommendation has recently been put forward regarding school-based smoking education programmes[56] and was an important theme in the Royal College of Physicians' report on teenage smoking.[2]

Further research is still required to find more effective approaches to developing personal skills in alcohol use. Based on more recent and advanced behavioural change theories, and on experience from other areas of health education, the most promising areas appear to be those summarised in Table 4.

Reorienting health services

Table 5 summarises the main intervention strategies that are recommended for reducing young people's drinking through reorienting health services.

This chapter has reviewed a range of approaches that might be used to prevent alcohol-related harm, particularly amongst children. There is no simple option or single strategy that dominates above others; indeed, the preoccupation with child-focused education and media campaigning has been singularly unimpressive. A synthesised and co-ordinated plan of action is needed to ensure the right mix of interventions directed at policy, education and services. Where this has been tried the results are much more encouraging.

Table 5
Recommended intervention strategies to reduce young people's drinking:

REORIENTING HEALTH SERVICES

❑ Strengthen the public advocacy role of health professionals and health authorities — for example through NAHAT (National Association of Health Authorities and Trusts), Directors of Public Health Medicine reports.

❑ Monitor and publish levels of alcohol misuse, smoking and drug use amongst young people at district level on a regular basis and encourage schools to do the same; monitor drinking rates in pregnancy.

❑ Emphasise the importance of the prevention of alcohol-related harm, as well as substance abuse in the work of all health care professionals.

❑ Accept responsibility for local, district and regional leadership and co-ordination of effective integrated control programmes for alcohol and other substances, and set up accountability and monitoring mechanisms.

❑ Ensure that health premises and health professionals, as well as teachers, set a good example for alcohol drinking and encourage colleagues who drink excessively to change.

Education strategies need to be entwined with environmental approaches to have any chance of effectiveness.[6]

To achieve this synergy of action requires leadership and resources at local, district, regional and national levels. The health services are ideally placed to offer such support, as indeed are teachers within the public and independent sectors.

The potential impact on the use of accident and emergency services by reducing alcohol problems alone should prompt serious review of whether the NHS is taking the prevention and control of alcohol misuse seriously enough.

Consequently, prevention is not a subject that should be relegated to a handful of poorly resourced and undervalued health educators. Rather, it should permeate the whole of the health service machinery and involve everyone in the service. All professional disciplines, particularly teachers, have a part to play at both primary and secondary care levels. Although there is a pervasive tendency within the caring professions to think only of action with individuals (usually after the harm has been caused), there is much they can do to stimulate and support a more health promoting environment. Raising community awareness and setting the public agenda is not only extremely valuable, but is also perfectly possible and cost-effective given the vast numbers working in the NHS.

Advocacy work then is particularly important for the NHS. More energetic and committed work is needed at a national level through the National Association of Health Authorities and Trusts (NAHAT), the national NHS health promotion agencies, non-governmental organisations such as Alcohol Concern as well as the Royal Medical Colleges. But advocacy can also take place at more local level within health authorities, for example, stimulated by the annual report of the District Director of Public Health Medicine.

Local information on the scale of alcohol misuse would help this process, but it is also needed to establish priorities, assist planning, set targets and monitor progress. Robust and repeatable surveys of young people's drinking have been found to be useful in winning political support and resources for health promotion investments. This should form part of the needs assessment tasks of all health authorities.

Work needs to start within the NHS itself. Emphasis should be given to ensuring that health premises and health professionals set a good example and that help is offered to members of staff who drink excessively. But increasingly, links and alliances should be formed with other organisations in the public, private and voluntary sectors to help them play their full part.

The NHS is limited in its effectiveness in that it does not pass laws, raise taxes, enforce environmental regulations, provide education services, etc. However, it can provide the legitimacy and incentives for others to act. New and innovative mechanisms for such intersectoral action should be tried and tested. It is true that we do not yet know how the health services can best play their part, but we have a good idea how they can do better. Further research and development work is urgently required and this will be discussed in Chapter 7.

6 Implications for training and education of professionals

Introduction

Professionals from a wide range of disciplines are in touch with parents who are problem drinkers, and with children and young people who are themselves either drinking over the recommended adult limits or at risk in other ways.

The training currently received by these professionals both at pre-qualification and post-qualification level on matters relevant to alcohol and substance abuse is very variable. A recent report of a Working Group set up to examine the training of staff who work with people with alcohol problems provides valuable information on this issue[1], and in what follows we have drawn heavily on its findings.

Training and education: the existing situation

Nurses

The role of nurses in the management of problem drinking and other substance misuse is likely to increase over the next decade, especially in response to the targets on drugs and alcohol outlined in the Government's 'Health of the Nation' document. Evidence from both the UK and the US suggests that nurse training currently fails to equip nurses with adequate knowledge.[2-5] For example, Watson[5] found that of 186 nurses working in six hospitals in Glasgow, half did not know the recommended safe limits for alcohol consumption. Nurses attributed their lack of knowledge and skills in this area of work to inadequate training. Arneson et al[3] found that most knowledge gained by American nurses was obtained through experience and self-directed learning, rather than formal nursing education. Among school nurses in the US, lack of knowledge and relevant skill were found to be the main deterrents in dealing with difficulties experienced by children of problem drinking parents.[2] It is likely that a similar situation exists in the UK.

One encouraging trend is that recently the English National Board (ENB) for Nursing, Midwifery and Health Visiting has appointed a Project Officer for substance misuse training who has a remit to research the current state of education relating to substance misuse education in all spheres of nursing. Nursing education requirements in this field have been detailed by Hicken.[6] As far as parents and the young are concerned, health visitors and school nurses are probably the groups most in need of training in this area.

Doctors

The Medical Council on Alcoholism has taken a lead in promoting education for medical students and doctors in this field. However, only sketchy information is available on the amount and effectiveness of training. The data that are available are not encouraging. For example, Farrell and David[7] found that 21% of psychiatric registrars failed to obtain details about the alcohol consumption of patients recently admitted. This compared to 39% among junior hospital doctors dealing with general admissions.[8]

A Department of Health Report[9] concluded 'the need for medical students to have basic information on alcohol misuse is accepted, and it is possible to identify a particular corpus of knowledge which should be given'. However, there does not appear to be any follow-up to indicate how far this recommendation has been implemented. Apart from general practitioners and specialists in substance abuse, the groups of doctors most in need of such information are hospital and community paediatricians, child and adolescent psychiatrists, and general psychiatrists.

Social workers

The Central Council for Education and Training in Social Work (CCETSW) has concerns about the inadequate level of professional education and training in relation to alcohol problems. In 1989 a national Department of Health/CCETSW survey of social work qualifying courses found that 11% of those that responded provided no training on substance problems.[10]

To address this, a curriculum development programme was initiated and guidance notes were produced, offering advice on how alcohol and other drug training is best approached. It emphasises the importance of confidentiality and harm minimisation and specifies what knowledge and skills social workers need to demonstrate at the completion of their qualifying training.

Children in residential care establishments are particularly likely to be at risk of excessive alcohol use. A recent local authority circular[11] provides helpful guidelines on attitudes of staff concerning alcohol consumption by young people, and the consumption by members of staff themselves.

Other groups of professionals

The report of the Working Party on Training of Staff who work with people with alcohol problems[1] describes the current training situation and makes recommendations in relation to the training of other groups concerned with children and young people. These include teachers, the police, probation officers, youth workers, psychotherapists and clinical psychologists. Although this Working Group did not specifically address training in relation to alcohol and the young, much of the information obtained was relevant to this age group. It is clear that there are many gaps in relation to education and training in all these groups.

The action required

Responsibility for establishing criteria and monitoring the nationwide adequacy of professional training lies with the bodies accrediting such training, including the General Medical Council, the General Nursing Council and the Central Council for the Education and Training of Social Workers, as well as the various bodies connected with the Royal Colleges. The training establishments, such as medical schools and schools of nursing have responsibility for implementing the requirements for training set by these bodies.

A number of organisations particularly TACADE, the voluntary body specifically focusing on training in alcohol and drug education, already produce useful material. The Health Education Authority and the Portman Group have both carried out a number of training projects and indeed we have heard from a wide range of other voluntary and statutory bodies concerned with alcohol education. The challenge is to ensure that training in this field does actually occur, and is of appropriate volume and quality.

We recommend that a common core training programme on alcohol issues should be included in basic training for all health, social and allied professionals. This programme should aim to give a basic understanding of alcohol, alcohol problems and show how professional skills can be applied to enable others to consider their own drinking behaviour.

Such a programme should include:

- An understanding of the way alcohol works and its physical, psychological and social effects, including the impact of parental drinking on children and adolescents.

- Self-awareness of one's own use and attitudes towards alcohol.

- How to recognise that a person may have drink problems, including a knowledge of the recommended limits for adults and their applicability to the young.

- An understanding of addiction and dependence and how people need or rely on alcohol.

- How to raise the issue of harmful drinking with teenagers and help them to make changes to their drinking.

- The effectiveness of interventions.

- Basic counselling skills in relation to parents and young people.

- Harm reduction.

- The legal aspects of alcohol.

- Information on local specialist alcohol services and when to refer on to those agencies.

In addition to the core training each profession will require specific education on alcohol that relates to its responsibilities:

Doctors:	— medical diagnoses that may be linked to alcohol consumption.
	— diagnostic tests that may be linked to alcohol consumption.
	— medication — detoxification, interactions with alcohol.
	— detoxification management.
Nurses:	— diagnosis linked to alcohol consumption.
	— nursing care during detoxification.
Social workers:	— implications of the Children Act and alcohol.

All those responsible for training professionals need to bear the following considerations in mind:

- In addition to receiving an alcohol training programme during their basic training, professionals require ongoing alcohol education to keep their knowledge and skills of the core programme current, and to add knowledge and skills as their professional role develops.

- Ongoing monitoring of training and training needs to be the responsibility of each professional group.

- Adequate funding for the core training and ongoing training is essential.

- Motivation to learn will be increased by including examination questions around the topic of alcohol.

- Responsibility for different aspects of training should be clearly assigned.

- Training should include an understanding of the need for organisational arrangements to help those professionals who may themselves develop problems with alcohol.

- Training should include establishment of policies around alcohol for staff and clients/patients/service users.

7 Research and development

Research activity into alcohol-related problems is at a low ebb in the UK. This is despite the fact that alcohol consumption directly or indirectly affects the lives of large numbers of children and young people, leads to major and widespread health problems in adults, and that there is much we do not know about the development, prevention and treatment of problem drinking. There are two major centres:

1 The Alcohol Research Group, in the Department of Psychiatry, University of Edinburgh is core-supported by the Portman Group, an independent company established in 1989 by the eight leading UK drinks companies. This centre obtains grant support from a wide variety of sources and carries out much research relevant to children and young people.

2 The Addiction Research Unit at the Institute of Psychiatry, University of London, has core support from central university funds, and also obtains grant support from other sources, especially the Medical Research Council.

Although relevant alcohol research is undertaken in other smaller centres, it is our impression that this is generally patchy and suffers from failure to reach a critical mass of scientific activity. Such problems relating to medical and socio-medical research in the UK are, of course, widespread and by no means confined to this field.

Funded by the Portman Group, a helpful compilation of alcohol research activity has been published by the Alcohol Research Group.[1] It reveals some interesting work but, in addition, a particular paucity of epidemiological studies investigating young people, a virtual absence of longitudinal studies and a deplorable lack of controlled intervention studies in relation to prevention or treatment. In line with the strategy outlined by the NHS Research and Development Section, Department of Health, we would recommend that initiatives should be taken to fill these gaps.

Sources of research funding

We should also comment on the fact that an increasing proportion of UK alcohol research is now funded directly or indirectly by the drinks industry. As well as the Portman Group, research is also supported directly by Whitbread PLC, by the Brewers' Society, and by the Scotch Whisky Association. All these bodies indicate that the research they support is independently conducted and that they exert no influence on the publication of results. We recognise that much research supported by the drinks industry, particularly that carried out by the Alcohol Research Group, is of high quality.

Nevertheless, we do think the present funding position in relation to the drinks industry is regrettable. In our view it is quite unavoidable that researchers funded by the drinks industry will tend to choose topics which will not result in harm to the industry, whatever the findings. As examples, we suggest that it is unlikely that the drinks industry would be requested to fund research leading to conclusions that more stringent taxation would be desirable, or that alcohol-free clubs and other leisure centres could be created, or that alcohol marketing policies and advertising regulations should be more tightly controlled.

An expanded research programme

We therefore recommend that the policy of allowing the drinks industry to make donations to independent research organisations should not be allowed to dominate the pattern of research activity. While we would be sad to see a decline in independent research supported by the drinks industry, we believe that many more programme and project grants in this area need to be supported by the major funding bodies, and that there is a need for the establishment of at least one major independent research centre for the investigation of alcohol and illicit drug problems in the young.

Further, there is a need for a more pro-active policy on the part of funding bodies, particularly the NHS Directorate of Research and Development, Regional Research Directorates, the Medical Research Council and Wellcome Trust to promote research in this field by centres already engaged in investigating normative and problem behaviours in children and young people.

We recommend that the NHS Research and Development Directorate should initiate a discussion meeting to establish how research in this neglected and important field could be promoted. Although this is an area in which cross-national research is very informative, it is not one in which one can rely on findings derived from other countries with different alcohol cultures and different attitudes towards the socialisation of the young.

There is no lack of topics in which important data are needed. Areas in which further enquiry is particularly needed include:

- Studies to clarify the relationship between drinking patterns in the young and subsequent development of drinking problems in adulthood.

- Studies to clarify the relationship between alcohol consumption and violent crime.

- Critical appraisal of the literature and further research to determine whether there is a need to formulate sensible limits of alcohol consumption specifically for young people.

- Studies to evaluate the effectiveness of interventions at the individual and population level in this age group.

- Studies to identify the relationship between alcohol consumption in the young and the use of tobacco and illicit drugs.

- Studies of drinking patterns in ethnic minorities, especially in second and third generation children and young people.

- Development of screening methods and intervention techniques suitable for young people who have drinking problems.

Rather than launching a series of small-scale research projects, it would be far preferable if a co-ordinated UK research strategy in this field were to be developed.

APPENDIX 1
The law relating to young people and alcohol

The complicated licensing laws seek to criminalise under-age drinking but they are extremely difficult to enforce. Moreover, since there are numerous exceptions to these provisions, for example, the fact that under-age drinking is perfectly lawful in registered clubs, the law presents a confusing message to teenagers.[1] Table A1 below sets out the legal provisions applying to children of differing ages.[2]

There are no legal provisions regulating the consumption of alcohol by young people over the age of 18 years. This is consistent with most other legislation, which reflects a view that a young person achieves complete autonomy on his eighteenth birthday, the age of attaining his legal majority.[3]

It is interesting to note that the law makes no attempt to regulate the provision of alcohol to children over the age of 5 years in private

Table A1
Laws relating to access to clubs and licensed premises for persons under 18 years

AGE	PROVISION
Any age	May be present in registered private members' clubs
Under 14	May not be present in the bar of licensed premises during permitted hours (S168 of the Licensing Act 1964), unless accompanied by a person over 18 and there is in force a children's certificate relating to the bar (Licensing Act 1964, s.3A, as inserted by s.19(1) of the Deregulation and Contracting Out Act 1994).
14+	May be in the bar of licensed premises during permitted hours.
Under 18	May not be employed in a bar of licensed premises when it is open for the sale or consumption of intoxicating liquor (S170 of 1964 Act), may not sell alcohol for consumption off the premises unless supervised by an adult (S171A of the 1964 Act).

Table A2
Laws relating to the purchase and consumption of alcohol for persons under 18 years

AGE	PROVISION
Under 5	May not be given alcohol except on medical orders (S5 Children and Young Persons Act 1933).
5+	May consume alcohol at home or in registered private members' clubs, or in any public place (subject to local bye-laws).
5+	May consume alcohol in an eating area on licensed premises if bought by an accompanying adult.
16+	May purchase beer, porter, cider or perry with a meal in an eating area or licensed premises (S169(4) of the Licensing Act 1964).
Under 18	May not purchase or be supplied with or consume alcohol in a bar (S169 of the Licensing Act 1964).
Under 18	May not purchase alcohol from an off licence, including supermarkets, or wholesaler (S169 of Licensing Act 1964).

homes, registered private clubs or any private places; instead its main objective is to prevent children consuming alcohol on licensed premises. There is therefore no specific alcohol related offence with which an adult could be charged, for example, for encouraging his or her child to consume alcohol in large quantities in their own home, though clearly the civil law would allow intervention to protect a child from such a parent. Nor is it an offence for any child within that age range to consume alcohol anywhere other than in licensed premises, for example at home or at school, or even in a registered club, however severely his health and education would suffer as a result.

In addition to the legislative provisions referred to in Tables A1 and A2, the licensing legislation also aims to make adults criminally liable for supplying alcohol to children in licensed premises. Consequently, there are extensive provisions which prohibit anyone selling intoxicating liquor in licensed premises to persons under 18, or allowing persons under 18 to consume such liquor in a bar, or anyone buying such liquor for consumption in a bar by a person under 18. Since implementation of the Licensing Act 1988, it is no longer necessary to prove knowledge that the teenager is under 18 before a conviction can be obtained[5] against an adult for selling alcohol to such a teenager. Nevertheless, it is a defence[6] for the person charged to prove that he exercised all due diligence to avoid committing the offence or that he had no reason to suspect that the person was under 18.

New legislation[7] has relaxed the general prohibition on the admission of children under 14 to the bars of licensed premises in England and Wales. The legislation empowers the licensing justices to grant, on application, 'children's certificates' for certain bar premises, on being satisfied that they provide a suitable environment for children under 14 accompanied by persons over 18, and that meals and non-alcoholic drinks are available in the certificated areas.

Definitions of problem drinking

(based on previously published definitions — the sources for which are given at the end of each section)

■ **Alcohol abuse:** A mal-adaptive pattern of use leading to clinically significant impairment or distress. It is indicated by one or more of the following:

a   Failure to fulfil major obligations at work, school or in the home.

b   Recurrent use of alcohol when it is physically hazardous (eg drinking and driving).

c   Recurrent alcohol-related legal problems, and

d   Continued use despite persistence of recurrent social or interpersonal problems caused or exacerbated by alcohol.

[American Psychiatric Association. Reproduced in abridged form from: *Diagnostic and statistical manual of mental disorders, 4th edn, revised.* (APA, Washington, DC, 1994.]

■ **Drug abuse:** Persistent or sporadic excessive drug use inconsistent with, or unrelated to acceptable medical practice.

■ **Drug misuse:** Any taking of a drug which harms or threatens to harm the physical or mental health or social well-being of an individual, of other individuals, or of society at large, or which is illegal.

[Royal College of Psychiatrists *Drug scenes: A report on drugs and drug dependence by the Royal College of Psychiatrists.* London: Gaskell, 1987.]

■ **Drug (alcohol) dependence:** A state, psychic and sometimes also physical, resulting from the interaction between a living organism and a drug, characterised by behavioural and other responses, that always includes a compulsion to take the drug on a continuous or sporadic basis in order to experience its psychic effects, sometimes to avoid the discomfort of abstinence. Tolerance may or may not be present. A person may be dependent on more than one drug.

The World Health Organisation use the following criteria:

- a subjective awareness of compulsion to use a drug or drugs, usually during attempts to stop or moderate drug use.

- a desire to stop drug use in the face of continued use.

- a relatively stereotyped drug-taking habit, ie a narrowing of the repertoire of drug-taking behaviour.

- evidence of neuro-adaptation (tolerance and withdrawal symptoms).

- the use of the drug to relieve or avoid withdrawal symptoms.

- the salience of drug-seeking behaviour relative to other important priorities.

- a rapid reinstatement of the syndrome after a period of abstinence.

[Edwards G, Gross M. Alcohol dependence: provisional description of a clinical description. *British Medical Journal* 1976;1:1058–61. Note: the WHO criteria are based on the defintions set out in this paper.]

■ **Unsanctioned use:** Use of a drug that is not approved by a society, or a group within society.

■ **Hazardous use:** Use of a drug that will probably lead to harmful consequences for the user, either to dysfunction or to harm.

■ **Dysfunctional use:** Use of a drug that is leading to impaired psychological or social functioning.

■ **Harmful use:** Use of a drug that is known to have caused tissue damage or mental illness in the particular person.

[Edwards G, Arif A, Hodgeson R. Nomenclature and classification of drug and alcohol related problems: a WHO memorandum. *Bulletin of World Health Organisation.* 1981;59: 225-42.]

■ **Harmful use:** A pattern of psychoactive substance use that is causing damage to health. The damage may be physical or mental.

[World Health Organisation. *The ICD-10 Classification of mental and behavioural disorders: clinical descriptions and diagnostic guidelines.* Geneva: WHO, 1992.

APPENDIX 3
List of helpful addresses

Alcohol Concern
   Waterbridge House
   32–36 Loman Street
   London SE1 0EE
   Tel: 0171 928 7377

Young Minds
   22 Boston Place
   London NW1 6ER
   Tel: 0171 724 7262

National Children's Bureau
   8 Wakley Street
   London EC1V 7QE
   Tel: 0171 843 6000

TACADE
   1 Hulme Place
   The Crescent
   SALFORD M5 4QA
   Tel: 0161 745 8925

References

Preface

1. Royal College of Physicians. *A great and growing evil: the medical consequences of alcohol abuse.* London: Tavistock, 1987.

2. Royal College of Psychiatrists. *Alcohol: our favourite drug.* London: Tavistock, 1986.

3. Royal College of General Practitioners. *Alcohol: a balanced view.* Report from General Practice No. 24. London: RCGP, 1986.

4. Royal College of Physicians, Royal College of Psychiatrists, Royal College of General Practitioners. *Alcohol and the heart in perspective: sensible limits reaffirmed.* Report of a joint working group. 1995.

Chapter 1 *Problem drinking by parents*

1. Royal College of Physicians. *A great and growing evil: the medical consequences of alcohol abuse.* London: Tavistock, 1987.

2. Morgan MY. The effects of moderate alcohol consumption on male fertility. In: Langer M, Chiandussi L, Chopra J, Martini L (eds). *The endocrines and the liver.* Serono Symposium No. 51. London: Academic Press, 1982: 157–8.

3. Nordberg L, Rydelius PA, Zetterström R. Children of alcoholic parents: health, growth, mental development and psychopathology until school age. *Acta Paediatrica Supplement* 1993;**387**: 1–24.

4. Harlap S, Shiono PH. Alcohol, smoking and incidence of spontaneous abortions in the first and second trimester. *Lancet* 1980;**ii**:173–6.

5. Day NI, Jasperse D, Richardson G, Robles N, *et al.* Prenatal exposure to alcohol: effect on infant growth and morphologic characteristics. *Pediatrics* 1989;**84**:536–41.

6. Opinion Research Corporation. *Public perceptions of alcohol consumption and pregnancy.* Study No. 33710. Princeton, USA: ORC, 1979.

7. Sokol RJ, Miller SI, Reed G. Alcohol abuse during pregnancy: an epidemiological study. *Alcoholism: Clinical and Experimental Research* 1980;**4**:135–45.

8. Halmesmäki E, Autti I, Granström M, Heikinheimo M, *et al.* Alpha-fetoprotein, human placental lactogen and pregnancy-specific beta-l-glycoprotein in pregnant women who drink: relation to fetal alcohol syndrome. *American Journal of Obstetrics and Gynecology* 1986;**155**:598–602.

9. Abel EL. *Fetal alcohol syndrome and fetal alcohol effects.* New York: Plenum Press, 1984.

10. Abel EL, Sokol RJ. Incidence of fetal alcohol syndrome and economic impact of FAS-related anomalies. *Drug and Alcohol Dependence* 1987;**19**: 51–70.

11. Cragg B, Singh S. Is ethanol a neurotoxin? In: Chubb IW, Giffen IB (eds). *Neurotoxins: fundamental and clinical advances.* Adelaide: Adelaide University Union Press, 1979:183–9.

12. Spohr H-L, Willms J, Steinhausen H-C. Prenatal alcohol exposure and long-term developmental consequences: a 10-year follow-up study of 60 children with fetal alcohol syndrome. *Lancet* 1993;**341**:907–10.

13. Streissguth AP, Clarren SK, Jones KL. Natural history of the fetal alcohol syndrome: a 10-year follow-up of 11 patients. *Lancet* 1985;**ii**:85–91.

14. Steinhausen H-C, Willms J, Spohr H-L. Long-term psychopathological and cognitive outcome of children with fetal alcohol syndrome. *Journal of the American Academy of Child and Adolescent Psychiatry* 1993;**32**:990–4.

15. Spohr H-L, Steinhausen H-C. Clinical, psychopathological and developmental aspects in children with the fetal alcohol syndrome: a four year follow-up study. In: *Mechanisms of alcohol damage in utero.* CIBA Foundation Symposium No. 105. London: Pitman, 1984:197–217.

16. MacDonald DR, Blume SB. Children of alcoholics. *American Journal of Diseases of Children* 1986;**140**:750–4.

17. Sher KJ. *Children of alcoholics: a critical appraisal of theory and research.* Chicago: University of Chicago Press, 1991.

18. West MO, Prinz RJ. Parental alcoholism and childhood psychopathology. *Psychological Bulletin* 1987;**102**:214–8.

19. Vaillant GE. Some differential effects of genes and environment on alcoholism. In: Rose RM, Barrett JE (eds). *Alcoholism: origins and outcome.* New York: Raven Press, 1988:75–82.

20. O'Connor MJ, Sigman M, Brill N. Disorganisation of attachment in relation to maternal alcohol consumption. *Journal of Consulting and Clinical Psychology* 1987;**55**:831–6.

21. Bernardi E, Jones M, Tennant C. Quality of parenting in alcoholics and narcotic addicts. *British Journal of Psychiatry* 1989;**154**:677–82.

22. von Knorring A-L. Children of alcoholics. *Journal of Child Psychology and Psychiatry* 1991; **32**: 411–21.

23. Reich W, Earls F, Frankel O, Shayka JJ. Psychopathology in children of alcoholics. *Journal of the American Academy of Child and Adolescent Psychiatry* 1993;**32**:995–1002.

24. Nylander I. Children of alcoholic fathers. *Acta Paediatrica Scandinavica* 1960;**49**: Suppl 121.

25. Velleman R, Orford J. The adult adjustment of offspring of parents with drinking problems. *British Journal of Psychiatry* 1993;**162**:503–16.

26. National Children's Home. *The hidden victims: children and domestic violence.* London: National Children's Home, 1994.

27. Mayhew WP, Maung NA, Mirrlees-Black C. *The 1992 British Crime Survey.* London: HMSO, 1993.

28. Skuse D, Bentovim A. Physical and emotional maltreatment. In: Rutter M, Taylor E, Hersov LA (eds). *Child and adolescent psychiatry.* Oxford: Blackwell Scientific Publications, 1994:209–29.

29. Creighton SJ. Personal communication based on 1988–90 NSPCC maintained child protection registers. London: NSPCC.

30. Oliver JE. Successive generations of child maltreatment: social and medical disorders in the parents. *British Journal of Psychiatry* 1985;**147**:484–90.

31. Leonard K, Jacob T. Alcohol, alcoholism and family violence. In: Van Hasselt V, Morrison R, Bellack A, Hersen M (eds). *Handbook of family violence.* New York: Plenum Press, 1988:383–406.

32. Chasnoff IJ. Drug use in pregnancy: parameters of risk. *Pediatric Clinics of North America* 1988;**35**:1403–12.

33. Smith M, Bentovim A. Sexual abuse. In: Rutter M, Taylor E, Hersov LA (eds). *Child and adolescent psychiatry.* Oxford: Blackwell Scientific Publications, 1994:230–51.

34. Yellowlees PM, Kaushik AV. The Broken Hill psychopathology project. *Australian and New Zealand Journal of Psychiatry* 1992;**26**:197–207.

35. Levene S, of the Child Accident Prevention Trust. Personal communication.

36. US Department of Transportation. *Traffic safety facts 1992.* Washington DC: National Center for Statistics and Analysis, 1993.

37. Department of Transport. *Accident fact sheet. Series 2, No.4.* London: Department of Transport, 1993.

Chapter 2 Assessment and management of children of problem drinking parents

1. Swadi H. Parenting capacity and substance misuse: an assessment scheme. *Association of Child Psychology and Psychiatry Newsletter* 1994;**16**:237–44.

2. Department of Health. *Guidelines on medical responsibility.* Provided by Department of Health, British Medical Association and Conference of Medical Royal Colleges. London: DoH, 1994.

3. Department of Health. *Working together with the Children Act 1989.* London: HMSO, 1991.

4. Kelleher K, Chaffin M, Hollenberg J, Fischer E. Alcohol and drug disorders among physically abusive and neglectful parents in a community-based sample. *American Journal of Public Health* 1994;**84**:1586–90.

Chapter 3 *Patterns of drinking behaviour in the young: prevalence, influences and impact*

1. Health Education Authority. *Tomorrow's young adults: 9–15 year olds look at alcohol, drugs, exercise and smoking.* London: HEA, 1992.

2. Office of Population Censuses and Surveys. *Adolescent drinking.* London:HMSO, 1986.

3. Mayhew WP, Maung NA, Mirrlees-Black C. *The 1992 British Crime Survey.* London: HMSO, 1993.

4. Department of Transport. *Accident fact sheet. Series 2, No. 4.* London: Department of Transport, 1993.

5. Brent D, Perper J, Goldstein CE, Kolko DJ, *et al.* Risk factors for adolescent suicide: a comparison of adolescent suicide victims with suicidal inpatients. *Archives of General Psychiatry* 1988;**45**:581–8.

6. Marsh A, *et al. Adolescent drinking.* Survey carried out on behalf of the Department of Health & Social Security and the Scottish Home & Health Department. Office of Population Censuses and Surveys. London: HMSO, 1986.

7. Health Education Authority. *Today's young adults: 16–19 year olds look at alcohol, drugs, exercise and smoking.* London: HEA, 1992.

8. Ghodsian M, Power C. Alcohol consumption between the ages of 16 and 23 in Britain: a longitudinal study. *British Journal of Addiction* 1987; **82**:175–80.

9. Plant MA, Peck DF, Stuart R. Self-reported drinking habits and alcohol-related campaigns amongst a cohort of Scottish teenagers. *British Journal of Addiction* 1982;**77**:75–90.

10. Smith C, Moore L, Wold B, Catford J. Health behaviours in school children: findings from the WHO cross-national study. In: APEE (ed). *Prevention of degenerative adult diseases: paediatric and educational aspects.* Rome: Universita degli Studi di Roma 'La Sapienza', 1993.

11. King AJC, Coles B. *Views and behaviours of 11, 13 and 15 year olds from 11 countries.* Ottawa: Ministry of National Health and Welfare, 1992.

12. Foxcroft DR, Lowe G, Alvarez JF, Weill J. *Adolescent drinking and family life in Europe: a pilot study.* Report to the Alcohol Education and Research Council. London, 1995.

13. Edwards G, Anderson P, Babor T, Casswell T, *et al. Alcohol policy and the public good.* Oxford: Oxford University Press, 1994.

14. Power C, Estaugh V. The role of family formation and dissolution in shaping drinking behaviour in early adulthood. *British Journal of Addiction* 1990;**85**:521–30.

15. Silbereisen RK, Robins L, Rutter M. Social trends in substance abuse: concepts and data on the impact of social change on alcohol and drug abuse. In: Rutter M, Smith D (eds). *Psychosocial disorders in young people: time, trends and their causes.* Chichester: Wiley, 1955

16. Orford J, Velleman R. Influence of parental drinking problems on drinking patterns of offspring. *British Journal of Addiction* 1990;**85**:779–94.

17. Green G, Macintyre S, West P, Ecob R. Like parent, like child? Associations between drinking and smoking behaviour of parents and their children. *British Journal of Addiction* 1991;**86**:745–58.

18. Hawkins JD, Catalano RF, Miller JY. Risk and protective factors for alcohol and other drug problems in adolescence and early adulthood: implications for substance abuse prevention. *Psychological Bulletin* 1992; **112**:64–105.

19. Pickens RW, Svikis DS, McGue M, Lykken DT, *et al.* Heterogeneity in the inheritance of alcoholism: a study of male and female twins. *Archives of General Psychiatry* 1991;**48**:19–28.

20. Orford J, Harwin J (eds). *Alcohol and the family*. London: Croom Helm, 1982.

21. Lowe G, Foxcroft DR, Sibley D. *Adolescent drinking and family life*. Reading, Berks: Harwood Academic Publishers, 1993.

22. Roberts H, Dengler R, Burley J, Zamorski A. *Trent health lifestyle survey*. Report to Trent Regional Health Authority. University of Nottingham Department of Public Health Medicine and Epidemiology, 1994.

23. Coleman JC. *Relationships in adolescence*. London: Routledge & Kegan Paul, 1974.

24. Plant MA, Plant ML. *Risk-takers: alcohol, drugs, sex and youth*. London: Tavistock, Routledge, 1992.

25. Swadi H. Substance use among 333 London adolescents. *British Journal of Addiction* 1988;**83**:935–42.

26. Pikkarainen PH, Raiha NCR. Development of alcohol dehydrogenase activity in the human liver. *Nature* 1969;**222**:563–4.

27. Gillam DM, Harper JR. Hypoglycaemia after alcohol ingestion. *Lancet* 1973;**1**:829–30.

28. Lamminpaa A, Vilska J, Korri U-M, Riihimaki V. Alcohol intoxication in hospitalised young teenagers. *Acta Paediatrica Scandinavica* 1993;**82**:773–8.

29. Cummins LH. Hypoglycaemia and convulsions in children following alcohol ingestion. *Journal of Pediatrics* 1961;**58**:23–6.

30. Hillbom M, Kaste M. Ethanol intoxication: a risk factor for ischemic brain infarction in adolescents and young adults. *Stroke* 1981;**12**:422–5.

31. Selbst SM, DeMaio JG, Doenning D. Mouthwash poisoning: report of a fatal case. *Clinical Pediatrics* 1986;**24**:162–3.

32. Beattie JO, Hull D, Cockburn F. Children intoxicated by alcohol in Nottingham and Glasgow, 1973-84. *British Medical Journal* 1986;**292**:519–21.

33. US Department of Transportation. *Traffic safety facts 1992*. Washington DC:National Center for Statistics and Analysis, 1993.

34. Transport and Road Research Laboratory. *The facts about drinking and driving*. Crowthorne, Berkshire,1983.

35. Department of Transport. *Road accidents in Great Britain.* London: HMSO, 1992.

36. Department of Transport. *Road accidents in Great Britain.* London: HMSO, 1984.

37. Hundleby J, Carpenter R, Ross R, Mercer G. Adolescent drug use and other behaviours. *Journal of Child Psychology and Psychiatry* 1982;**23**:61–8.

38. Deykin E, Levy J, Wells V. Adolescent depression, alcohol and drug abuse. *American Journal of Public Health* 1987;**77**:178–82.

39. Fowler R, Rich C, Young D. San Diego suicide study: substance abuse in young cases. *Archives of General Psychiatry* 1986;**43**:962–5.

40. James I. Suicide and mortality among heroin addicts in Britain. *British Journal of Addiction* 1967;**62**:391–8.

41. Weissman M, Pottenger M, Kleber H. Symptom patterns in primary and secondary depression. *Archives of General Psychiatry* 1977;**34**:854–62.

42. Diekstra RF. Suicidal behaviour in adolescents and young adults. *Crisis* 1989;**10**:16–35.

43. Hawton K, Fagg J, Platt S, Hawkins M. Factors associated with suicide after parasuicide in young people. *British Medical Journal* 1993;**306**:1641–4.

44. Lavik N, Onstad S. Drug use and psychiatric symptoms in adolescence. *Acta Psychiatrica Scandinavica* 1986;**73**:437–40.

45. Labouvie E. Alcohol and marijuana use in relation to adolescent stress. *International Journal of the Addictions* 1986;**21**:333–45.

46. Collins J (ed). *Drinking and crime: perspectives on the relationship between alcohol consumption and criminal behaviour.* New York: Guilford Press, 1981.

47. West R, Drummond C, Eames K. Alcohol consumption, problem drinking and anti-social behaviour in a sample of college students. *British Journal of Addiction* 1990;**85**:479–86.

48. Home Office Standing Conference on Crime Prevention. *Young people and alcohol.* Report of working group. London: Home Office, 1987.

49. Fagan J, Weis J, Cheng Y. Delinquency and substance use among inner-city students. *Journal of Drug Issues* 1990;**20**:351–402.

50. Hammersley R, Forsyth A, Lavelle T. The criminality of new drug users in Glasgow. *British Journal of Addiction* 1990;**85**:1583–94.

51. Kingery P, Pruitt B, Hurley R. Violence and illegal drug use among adolescents: evidence from the US National Adolescent Student Health Survey. *International Journal of the Addictions* 1992;**27**:1445–64.

52. Fehrenbach P, Smith W, Monastersky C, Deisher R. Adolescent sexual offenders: offender and offense characteristics. *American Journal of Orthopsychiatry* 1986;**56**:225–33.

53. Kavoussi R, Kaplan M, Becker J. Psychiatric diagnoses in adolescent sex offenders. *Journal of the American Academy of Child and Adolescent Psychiatry* 1988;**27**:241–3.

54. Strunin L, Hingson R. Alcohol, drugs and adolescent sexual behaviour. *International Journal of the Addictions* 1992; **27**:129–46.

55. DiClemente R, Durbin M, Siegel D, Krasnovsky F, *et al.* Determinants of condom use among junior high school students in a minority, inner-city school district. *Pediatrics* 1992;**89**:197–202.

56. McEwan R, McCallum A, Bhopal R, Madhok R. Sex and the risk of HIV infection: the role of alcohol. *British Journal of Addiction* 1992;**87**:577–84.

57. Kandel D. Stages in adolescent involvement in drug use. *Science* 1975;**190**:912–4.

58. Kandel D, Faust R. Sequence and stages in patterns of adolescent drug use. *Archives of General Psychiatry* 1975;**32**:923–32.

59. Donovan J, Jessor R. Problem drinking and the dimension of involvement with drugs: a Guttman scalogram analysis of adolescent drug use. *American Journal of Public Health* 1983;**73**:543–52.

60. Kandel D, Yamaguchi K, Chen K. Stages of progression in drug involvement from adolescence to adulthood: further evidence for the gateway theory. *Journal of Studies on Alcohol* 1992;**53**:447–57.

61. Bailey S. Adolescents' multisubstance use patterns: the role of heavy alcohol and cigarette use. *American Journal of Public Health* 1992;**82**:1220–4.

62. Bagnall G. Use of alcohol, tobacco and illicit drugs amongst 13 year olds in three areas of Britain. *Drug and Alcohol Dependence* 1988;**22**:241–51.

63. Swadi H. *Epidemiological aspects of adolescent substance misuse in a population of London adolescents.* MPhil thesis, London University, 1988.

64. Parker H. Personal communication.

Chapter 4 Assessment and treatment of alcohol problems in the young

1. Health Advisory Service *Review of services for children and adolescents who misuse alcohol and other substances.* Sutton, Surrey: NHS Health Advisory Service. (In press.)

2. Department of Health. *Report of the Chief Medical Officer.* London: DoH, 1994.

3. Wallace P, Cremona A, Anderson P. Safe limits of drinking: general practitioners' views. *British Medical Journal* 1985;**290**:1875–6.

4. Anderson P. Managing alcohol problems in general practice. *British Medical Journal* 1985;**290**:1873–5.

5. Department of Health. *Guidelines on smoking and alcohol consumption in residential childcare establishments.* LAC 94(4). London: DoH, 1994.

6. Wallace P, Haines A. Use of questionnaires in general practice to increase the recognition of patients with excessive alcohol consumption. *British Medical Journal* 1985;**290**:1949–53.

7. Saunders J, Aasland O, Babor T, *et al.* Development of the Alcohol Use Disorder Identification Test (AUDIT): WHO collaborative project on early

detection of persons with harmful alcohol consumption. *Addiction* 1993; **88**:791–804.

8. Wallace P, Cutler S, Haines A. Randomised controlled trial of general practitioner intervention in patients with excessive alcohol consumption. *British Medical Journal* 1988;**297**:663–8.

9. Babor TF, Grant M. *Project on identification and management of alcohol-related problems. Report on phase II: a randomised clinical trial of brief interventions in primary health care.* Geneva: World Health Organisation, 1992.

10. Prochaska J, DiClemente C. Transtheoretical therapy: toward a more integrative model of change. *Psychotherapy: Theory, Research and Practice* 1982;**19**:276–88.

11. Brown S, Vik P, Creamer V. Characteristics of relapse following adolescent substance abuse treatment. *Addiction Behaviour* 1989;**14**:291–300.

12. Myers M, Brown S. Coping responses and relapse among adolescent substance abusers. *Journal of Substance Abuse* 1990;**2**:177–89.

13. Monti PM, Abrams DB, Binkoff JA, Zwick WR, *et al.* Communication skills training, communication skills training with family and cognitive behavioral mood management training for alcoholics. *Journal of Studies on Alcohol* 1990;**51**:263–70.

14. Fishman C, Stanton D, Rosman B. Treating families of substance abusing adolescents. In: Stanton M, Todd T (eds). *The family therapy of drug abuse and addiction.* New York: Guilford Press, 1982.

15. Bry B. Family-based approaches to reducing adolescent substance use: theories, techniques and findings. In: *Adolescent drug abuse: analyses of treatment research.* National Institute of Drug Abuse Research Monograph 77. Maryland:NIDA, 1988.

16. Cartwright A. Group work with substance abusers: basic issues and future research. *British Journal of Addiction* 1987;**82**:951–3.

Chapter 5 Prevention

1. World Health Organisation. Ottawa Charter for Health Promotion. *Health Promotion (International Journal)* 1987;**1**:4,i–v.

2. Royal College of Physicians. *Smoking and the young.* London: RCP, 1992.

3. Norström T. *Alcohol and damages: the aggregate evidence.*(in press).

4. Rusk B, Gliksman L, Brook R. Alcohol availability, alcohol consumption and alcohol-related damage. I. The distribution of consumption model. *Journal of Studies on Alcohol* 1986;**47**:1–10.

5. Lenke L. *Alcohol and criminal violence: time series analyses in a comparative perspective.* Stockholm: Almqvist and Wiksell International, 1990.

6. Edwards G, Anderson P, Babor T, Casswell T, *et al. Alcohol policy and the public good.* Oxford: Oxford University Press, 1994.

7. Sutton M, Godfrey C. *The Health of the Nation targets for alcohol: a study of the economic and social determinants of high alcohol consumption in different population groups.* Centre for Health Economics, University of York, 1994.

8. Strickland DE. Alcohol advertising: orientations and influence. *International Journal of Advertising* 1982;**1**:307–19.

9. Strickland DE. Advertising exposure, alcohol consumption and misuse of alcohol. In: Grant J, Plant M, Williams A (eds). *Economics and alcohol: consumption and controls.* New York: Gardner Press, 1983:201–22.

10. Atkin CK, Hocking J, Block M. Teenage drinking: does advertising make a difference? *Journal of Communication* 1984;**34**:157–67.

11. Atkin CK, Block M. The effects of alcohol advertising. In: Kinnear TC (ed). *Advances in consumer research.* Utah: Provo, Association for Consumer Research, 1984:688–93.

12. Grube JW, Wallack L. Television beer advertising and drinking knowledge, beliefs, and intentions among schoolchildren. *American Journal of Public Health* 1994;**84**:180–1

13. Connolly GM, Casswell S, Zang ZF. Silva PA. Alcohol in the mass media and drinking by adolescents: a longitudinal study. *Addiction 89* 1994; **89**(1255–63)

14. O'Malley PM, Wagenaar AC. Effects of minimum drinking age laws on alcohol use, related behaviours and traffic crash involvement among American youth: 1976–1987. *Journal of Studies on Alcohol* 1991;**52**:478–91.

15. US General Accounting Office. *Drinking-age laws: an evaluation synthesis of their impact on highway safety.* Washington, DC: US Superintendent of Documents, 1987.

16. Marsh A, *et al. Adolescent drinking.* Survey carried out on behalf of the Department of Health & Social Security and the Scottish Home & Health Department. Office of Population Censuses and Surveys. London: HMSO, 1986.

17. Sharp DL. Underage drinking in the United Kingdom since 1970: public policy, the law and adolescent drinking behaviour *Alcohol and Alcoholism* 1994;**29**:555–63.

18. Home Office. *Possible reforms of the liquor licensing system in England and Wales: a consultation paper.* London, 1993;para 2.15–2.16.

19. Drummond AE, Cave TC, Healy DJ. The risk of accident involvement by time of week: an assessment of the effects of zero BAC legislation and the potential of driving curfews. In: Benjamin T (ed). *Young drivers impaired by alcohol and other drugs.* London: Royal Society of Medicine Services, 1987:385–98.

20ᴬ Hingson R, Heeren T, Morelock S. Preliminary effects of Maine's 1982 0.02 law to reduce teenage driving after drinking. In: Benjamin T (ed). *Young drivers impaired by alcohol and other drugs.* London: Royal Society of Medicine Services, 1986:377–84.

20ᴮ Hingson R, Howland J, Morelock S, Heeren T. Legal interventions to reduce drunken driving and related fatalities among youthful drivers. *Alcohol, Drugs and Driving* 1988;4:87–98.

21. Homel R. *Policing and punishing the drinking driver: a study of general and specific deterrence.* New York: Springer-Verlag, 1988.

22. Arthurson R. *Evaluation of random breath testing.* Research Note RN10/85. Sydney: Traffic Authority of New South Wales, 1985.

23. Mathijssen R, Wesemann P. The role of police enforcement in the decrease of DWI in the Netherlands 1983-1991. In: Utzelmann H-D, Berghaus G, Kroj G (eds). *Alcohol, drugs and traffic safety.* T92, Band 3. Proceedings of 12th International Conference on Alcohol, Drugs and Traffic Safety, Sep 28–Oct 2 1992, Cologne, Germany, 1993.

24. Voas RB, Hause JM. Deterring the drinking driver: the Stockton experience. *Accident Analysis and Prevention* 1987;**19**:81–90.

25. Greenfield TK, Graves KL, Kaskulas LA. Alcohol warning labels for prevention: national survey findings. *Alcohol, Health and Research World* (in press).

26. Hankin JR, Sloan JJ, Firestone IJ, Ager JW, *et al.* A time series analysis of the impact of the alcohol warning label on antenatal drinking. *Alcoholism: Clinical and Experimental Research* 1993;**17**:284–9.

27. Hilton ME. *Perspectives and prospects in warning label research.* 18th Annual Alcohol Epidemiology Symposium, Toronto, 30 May–5 June 1992.

28. Amundesen A. Hva skjer når et vinutsalg åpnes? (What happens when a wine outlet is opened?) *Norsk Tidsskrift om Alkoholsp rsmålet* 1967;**19**:65–82.

29. Österberg E. Current approaches to limit alcohol abuse and the negative consequences of use: a comparative overview of available options and an assessment of proven effectiveness. In: Aasland O (ed). *The negative social consequences of alcohol use.* Oslo: Norwegian Ministry of Health and Social Affairs, 1991:266–9.

30. Denney J. Low alcohol beers and lagers and blood alcohol levels. In: *Alcohol, drugs and traffic safety* (see ref 23):1506–12.

31. Bruun K, Edwards G, Lumio M, Måkelå K, *et al. Alcohol control policies in public health perspective.* Helsinki: Finnish Foundation for Alcohol Studies 1975;25.

32. Godfrey C. Licensing and the demand for alcohol. *Applied Economics* 1988; **20**:1541–58.

33. Smith DI. Effect on casualty traffic accidents of the introduction of 10pm Monday to Saturday hotel closing in Victoria. *Australian Drug and Alcohol Review* 1988;**7**:163–6.

34. Olsson O, Wikstrom P-OH. Effects of the experimental Saturday closing of liquor retail stores in Sweden. *Contemporary Drug Problems* 1982;**11**:325–53.

35. Nordlund S. *Effects of Saturday closing of wine and spirit shops in Norway.* Paper presented at 31st International Institute on the Prevention and Treatment of Alcoholism, Rome, 2-7 June. National Institute for Alcohol Research, SIFA, Mimeograph No. 5/85, Oslo, 1985.

36. Säilä S-L. Lauantaisulkemiskokeilu ja Juopumushäiröt (A trial closure of Alko retail shops on Saturdays and disturbances caused by intoxication). *Alkoholpolitiikka* 1978;**43**:91–9.

37. Bruce D. Changes in Scottish drinking habits and behaviour following the extension of permitted evening opening hours. *Health Bulletin* 1980; **38**:133–7.

38. Saltz RF. The introduction of dram shop legislation in the United States and the advent of server training. *Addiction* 1993;**88**(Suppl):95S–103S.

39. Saltz RF, Hennessy M. *Reducing intoxication in commercial establishments: an evaluation of responsible beverage service practices.* Berkeley, California: Prevention Research Center, 1990.

40. Holder HD, Wagenaar AC. Mandated server training and the reduction of alcohol-involved traffic crashes: a time series analysis in the state of Oregon. *Accident Analysis & Prevention* (in press).

41. Holder HD, Janes K, Mosher J, Saltz R, *et al.* Alcoholic beverage server liability and the reduction of alcohol-involved problems. *Journal of Studies on Alcohol* 1993;**54**:23–36.

42. Wagenaar AC, Holder HD. Effects of alcohol beverage server liability on traffic crash injuries. *Alcoholism: Clinical and Experimental Research* 1991; **15**:942–7.

43. Casswell S, Gilmore L. An evaluated community action project on alcohol. *Journal of Studies on Alcohol* 1989;**50**:339–46.

44. Casswell S, Gilmore L, Maguire V, Ransom R. Changes in public support for alcohol policies following a community-based campaign. *British Journal of Addiction* 1989;**84**:515–22.

45. Gliksman L. Alcohol management policies for municipal recreation departments: an evaluation of the Thunder Bay model. In: Giesbrecht N, Cox A (eds). *Prevention and the environment.* Toronto: Addiction Research Foundation, 1986:198–204.

46. Hingson R, McGovern T, Heeren T, Winter M, Zakocs R. *Impact of the Saving Lives Program.* 19th Annual Alcohol Epidemiology Symposium, Krakow, Poland, June 1993.

47. Barber JG, Bradshaw R, Walsh C. Reducing alcohol consumption through television advertising. *Journal of Consulting and Clinical Psychology* 1989; **57**:613–8.

48. Comiti VP. The advertising of alcohol in France. *World Health Forum* 1990;**11**:242–5.

49. Wallack L, Barrows DC. Evaluating primary prevention: the California 'winners' alcohol program. *International Quarterly of Community Health Education* 1983;**3**:307–36.

50. Atkin CK. Mass communication effects on drinking and driving. In: *Surgeon General's workshop in drunk driving: background papers.* Washington, DC: US Department of Health and Human Services, 1989:15–34.

51. Pentz MA, Dwyer JH, MacKinnon DP, Flay BR, *et al.* A multicommunity trial for primary prevention of adolescent drug abuse: effects on drug use prevalence. *Journal of the American Medical Association* 1989;**261**:3259–66.

52. Hansen WB, Johnson CA, Flay BR, Graham JW, Sobel J. Affective and social influences approaches to the prevention of multiple substance abuse among seventh grade students: results from Project SMART. *Preventive Medicine* 1988;**17**:135–54.

53. Hansen WB, Graham JW, Wolkenstein BH, Lundy BZ, *et al.* Differential impact of three alcohol prevention curricula on hypothesized mediating variables. *Journal of Drug Education* 1988;**18**:143–53.

54. Gerstein D, Green L (eds). *Preventing drug abuse: what do we know?* Washington DC: National Academy Press, 1993.

55. Moskowitz JM. The primary prevention of alcohol problems: a critical review of the research literature. *Journal of Studies on Alcohol* 1989;**50**:54–88.

56. Nutbeam D, Smith C, Catford J. Evaluation of two smoking education programmes under normal classroom conditions. *British Medical Journal* 1993;**306**:102–7.

Chapter 6 Implications for training and education of professionals

1. Alcohol Concern. *A national training strategy.* London, 1992.

2. Arneson S, *et al.* Children of alcoholic parents: identification and intervention. *Children's Health Care* 1983;**11**(3):107–12.

3. Arneson S, Schultz M, Triplett J. Nurses' knowledge of the impact of parental alcoholism on children. *Archives of Psychiatric Nursing* 1987;**1**(4):251–7.

4. Friend B. Drink drive. *Nursing Times* 16 September 1992:**88**(38).

5. Watson H. *Identification and minimal intervention for at risk and early problem drinkers in general hospital wards: a role for nurses?* Glasgow: University of Strathclyde, 1992.

6. Hicken I. *Education and training for nurses working in the field of substance abuse.* Report. London: ENB, 1992.

7. Farrell M, David A. Do psychiatric registrars take a proper drinking history? *British Medical Journal* 1988;**296**:395–6.

8. Barrison I, Viola L, Murray-Lyon I. Do housemen take an adequate drinking history? *British Medical Journal* 1980;**281**:1040.

9. Department of Health. *Alcohol related problems in undergraduate medical education: a survey of English medical schools.* London: DoH, 1987.

10. Harrison L. *Alcohol and drugs education in social work qualifying training. Issues in Social Work Education* 1990;**10**:51–68

11. Department of Health. *Guidelines on smoking and alcohol consumption in residential childcare establishments.* LAC 94(4). London: DoH, 1994.

Chapter 7 Research and development

1. May C. *Research on alcohol education for young people: a critical review of the literature.* Alcohol Research Group, 1991.

Appendix 1 The law relating to young people and alcohol

1. Home Office Standing Conference on Crime Prevention. *Young people and alcohol.* Report of working group. London: Home Office, 1987: 20–3, 40–9.

2. Department of Health. *Guidelines on smoking and alcohol consumption in residential child care establishments.* LAC 94(4). London: DoH, 1994. Adopted from Appendix i, and amended to take account of the Deregulation and Contracting Out Act 1994, s19 and Schedule 7.

3. Family Law Reform Act 1969, s1.

4. For example a local authority might apply for a care order under section 31 Children Act 1989 authorising the removal of the child from his parents' care.

5. Under section 169(1) Licensing Act 1964.

6. Under section 169(4A) Licensing Act 1964.

7. Deregulation and Contracting Out Act 1994, section 19 (which amends section 168 of the Licensing Act 1964) and Schedule 7.